The Serenity Handbook

The Official Crew Member's Guide to the Firefly-Class Series 3 Ship

By Marc Sumerak

TITAN BOOKS

London

An Insight Editions Book

Welcome aboard Serenity, the finest ship to ever sail the black!

This old girl has seen plenty of action in these few years since the captain brought her back to life. More than most in her class were built to handle, I reckon. But thanks to the help of a dedicated crew (and Jayne), we've managed to keep her afloat. And she's done the same for us.

If you're plannin' on signin' on to this crew—and the fact that you're botherin' to read this book suggests that you may in fact be—you need to know that Serenity is more than just a ship. She's one of us. Family. And like us, she's got her good days and her bad, so understandin' what will make her engines purr again might make all the difference in the 'Verse when the Alliance is breathin' up our exhaust port.

That's why I decided to compile this here manual, to give anyone on board—passengers and crew members alike—the opportunity to get acquainted with Serenity's every nook and cranny. As it turns out, I ain't the only one who's got somethin' to say about our girl. The entire crew—from the captain to the Shepherd—chipped in to give their two credits. Thanks to them, you're guaranteed to have everythin' you need to know about how to fly her, how to fix her, and, most important, how to treat her right.

I'm sure there are fancier tech guides out there that'll tell you how to purge a clogged hydraulic line or which wrench you'll need to install a new catalyzer, but keepin' a ship runnin' is about more than just fixin' its parts. It's about healin' its soul.

That may not make sense yet, but once you get to know Serenity, it will. Hope you stick around long enough to find out why.

Stay shiny,

Kaylee

Serenity

Ship's Manual

by the crew

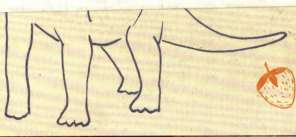

Contents

Contents

Welcome to Serenity

Ever meet someone for the first time but reckon you've known 'em for your entire life? That's how I felt, first I laid eyes on Serenity.

Ain't the only time I'd happened across a Series 3 Firefly, course. Seen plenty of 'em—the military kind—during the war. They raced through the skies to take arms 'gainst the Alliance and rained back through the atmo in pieces. They weren't designed to fight, but they tried hard as hell. No shame in that.

Maybe that's what drew me to this ship back when I spied her in that boneyard on Hera. She was a kindred spirit, willin' to fly high against all odds.

Whatever shape she was in, whoever had ridden her into the ground and left her for dead, don't matter much. Serenity may have just been a broken-down mid-bulk transport to the average eye, but I seen in her what no one else could—potential.

> Or it might've been 'cause she was tragically humped and desperate for love.
> —Zoë

> So, they are kindred spirits after all.
> —Inara

Ain't no secret a Firefly is a good, reliable ship, 'specially a Series 3. Book will tell you about the smooth ride. Kaylee will ramble on for hours about the upgraded engines. Even the Alliance will admit that this model is a smuggler's dream. That's all well and good, but ain't none of those the reasons why I chose her.

To me, Serenity aimed to be more than just a ride from one point of the 'Verse to another. She was a chance to regain everythin' we had been fightin' for. This boat would let us chart our own course. With the right crew, we could take jobs as we chose, never livin' under nobody's heel ever again.

She certainly ain't about to win no beauty contests. Then again, neither am I. But freedom? Can't say I've ever found anything prettier than that.

—Mal

BILL OF SALE

CLASSIFICATIONS:

CLASS: 03-K64 FIREFLY

TYPE: MID-BULK TRANSPORT (CLASS B)

REGISTRATION: U.A.P./HERA

REGISTRY NUMBER: 404-E-132-4FE274A

PULSE BEACON CODE: SUB-BAND 088.1101

MANUFACTURER:

- ALLIED SPACECRAFT CORP., OSIRIS
- FIREFLY SHIP WORKS, LTD., HERA
- MANDEL & EARLS, LTD., LONDINIUM

MANUFACTURER MODEL NO.: 47 MARK IV

HULL LAID: AUGUST 2459

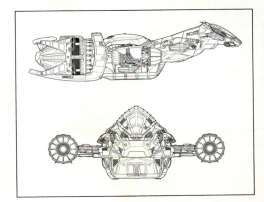

SPECIFICATIONS:

DRIVE: STANDARD RADION/ACCELERATOR CORE

STANDARD ACCELERATION: 4.2 G

SHIP LENGTH: 269' 3" (82.1 M)

SHIP WIDTH: 170' 0" (51.8 M)

SHIP HEIGHT: 78' 8" (24.0 M)

WEIGHT: 282,500 LB.
(128.1 METRIC TON)

MAX WEIGHT: 585,000 LB.
(265.4 METRIC TON)

MAX PAYLOAD: 164,900 LB.
(74.8 METRIC TON)

CAPACITY: 5 CREW/18 PASSENGERS

INCLUDED IN SALE:

ENDO-/EXO-ATMOSPHERIC SHUTTLES

CONDITION:

CURRENTLY NONOPERATIONAL

PURCHASE INFORMATION:

OWNER OR SHIP'S MASTER:
MALCOM REYNOLDS

PURCHASE PRICE (STANDARD CREDITS):
ON FILE

SHIP NAME (IF CHANGED): "SERENITY"

DATE OF TRANSFER: 16 JANUARY, 2512

Vehicles are sold "as-is" and all sales are final. Seller cannot be held responsible for any defects, missing parts, illegal modifications, or performance issues of the vehicle. Seller does not promise any type of guarantee or warranty, either expressly written or implied, and Buyer waives any right to take legal action against the Seller should the vehicle not pass Alliance inspection standards. Buyer agrees that Seller offers no other commitments or promises beyond the transfer of ownership of the vehicle itself. All sale records will be kept private and confidential, unless otherwise requested by the Alliance.

SIGNATURE:

Malcom Reynolds

DATE:

16 January 2515

Name's Malcolm Reynolds. Folks just call me Mal. You can call me Captain. Serenity is my boat, and if you're on board, you're under my command, plain and simple. That don't sit well with you, then you best be findin' another ship on which to sit.

Wasn't always out here, lost in the sky. Some time back, I had my boots planted firmly on the ground. But I was lost in something else—an idea. One much bigger than me that I reckoned was worth fightin' for. And boy, did I fight. S'pose that's the one thing I've always been good at. Winnin', on the other hand, that don't always come quite as natural.

Not for lack of tryin', sir. —Zoë

It might've been called the Unification War, but don't let that fool ya. It lasted for five long years and ripped the 'Verse apart along the way. When I marched into Serenity Valley, I had every intention of makin' sure that the war came to an end. Never crossed my mind it might mean layin' down my arms and handing the Alliance their victory. The Independent army was ordered to surrender that day, but I've never been one for fallin' in line. If the planets couldn't be free, I fathomed I'd go to the one place where I knew I could be. Out here.

Are any of us ever truly free? —Book

I KNOW INARA AIN'T. TRUST ME. I'VE INQUIRED. —JAYNE

For you, Jayne, I'd charge triple. —Inara

Back during the war, I was a sergeant, not a captain. But things ain't really all that different. Still have a group of loyal soldiers willin' to follow me to hell and back for one reason alone: to do what's right. Not just for us, but for them that's been wronged. Didn't learn that from the war. Learned it from my mother back on Shadow.

"CAPTAIN MAMA'S BOY." AIN'T THAT JUST PRECIOUS. —JAYNE

Not as precious as your hat. —Wash

You got a problem, I'll be aimin' to help much as I can. You become a problem, though, I'll be aimin' to end it—and maybe you—right quick, dǒng ma? Already got plenty problems myself, thank you kindly. But, after all I seen, maybe I should be glad I still got something I can call my own.

—Mal

CRIMINAL PROFILE: REYNOLDS, MALCOLM

尼仑丫九因边刀马, 叼兵让田叼

NAME: Malcolm Reynolds

GENDER: Male

DOB: 2468|09|20

SOCIAL CONTROL #:
099,836,5,4112

Son of a rancher, born on the planet Shadow.

HEIGHT: 6'2"

WEIGHT: 215 lbs.

HAIR: Brown

EYES: Blue

WAR RECORD:
Captain
Independent Army
57th Brigade
Volunteer

AWARDED VALOR COMMENDATION:
Battle of Serenity Valley

BOUND BY LAW FIVE TIMES:
- Smuggling
- Tariff dodging
- Transporting illegal cargo

NO CONVICTIONS.

SUSPECTED OF:
- Theft of Alliance goods
- Conspiring with known criminals
- Harboring fugitives

CURRENT OCCUPATION:
Captain, 03-K64-Firefly-Class Mid-Bulk Transport, "Serenity"

KNOWN ALIASES:
- "Captain Harbatkin"
- "Miles Arixoen, M.D."

KNOWN ASSOCIATES:
- Zoë Alleyne Washburne
- Hoban Washburne
- Jayne Cobb
- Kaywinnet Lee Frye
- Inara Serra (Registered Companion)
- Derrial Book (Shepherd)

SUSPECTED ASSOCIATES:
- Simon Tam—FUGITIVE
- River Tam—FUGITIVE

ALLIANCE PERSON OF INTEREST

CAUTION LEVEL:

EXTREMELY HIGH

STAFF
ST. LUCY'S MEDICAL CENTER

卡绘 尼因 叼岂 业业 身 番亚 闷治
强健

Miles Arixoen M.D.

013 | 强健 | 548
DEPARTMENT

强健

72382 | 3575878

FORMER SITE OF
BLUE SUN/UAP
ATMOSPHERE
PROCESSOR

SERENITY VIEW
TOWNSHIP

SEREN

SERENIDADE RIVER

VALLEY

Y VALLEY

WESTERN TIP OF
MERCER HOLLY
ORE VEINS

START OF BADLANDS

SENTINEL
DOME

EARTH THAT
WAS MEMORIAL

Hera

Serenity Valley

SERIES 1 *Firefly*

In the early days of the 'Verse, the Central Planets' trade routes were serviced by a combination of enormous freighters and short-range cargo transports. Once large numbers of settlers began to spread farther out toward the Rim, though, gettin' supplies to their colonies became quite the challenge. The massive freighters were too costly to operate, makin' long missions to deliver just a fraction of their load a guaranteed loss. Smaller ships were only meant for quick jumps, city-to-city or planet-to-moon, and couldn't handle the cargo or the crew needed for a lengthy trip out to a Border planet.

So the Central Planets left the Border worlds alone, and they all lived happily ever after, and we never had to sit through any of Mal's war stories. The end!
—Wash

Turns out, as independent as the new worlds wanted to be, they still couldn't survive without supplies. Out of necessity, the mid-bulk transport was born. This class of ships was designed for long-range travel but was scaled down to reflect the reduced cargo needs of these frontier worlds. Because of their smaller size, the ships could be easily maintained by a limited crew and operated on a significantly smaller budget. One of the sturdiest and most reliable of the bunch was built by the Allied Spacecraft Corporation and became known as the Firefly.

And the 'Verse was never the same.
—Mal

Each version of the Firefly, starting with the original Series 1 model that launched in 2435, shares the same signature features: dual engines that rotate for vertical takeoff and landing, a centralized cargo compartment, a raised bridge and crew deck at the fore, and the bulbous main reactor whose glow earned the ship her name. She may not have looked like much, but the Series 1 has since become the stuff of legends.

Hard to believe they only built eight thousand of 'em!
—Kaylee

However, the Series 1 Firefly lacked some of the important features we take for granted these days. There was no modular cargo area, no passenger rooms, the shuttles were extremely small, and the engines only had a limited range of rotation. But what the Series 1 did have was a solid foundation, one that would be built upon to get us where we are today.

— *Zoë*

BASED ON OUR RECENT DESTINATIONS, I AIN'T SURE I SHOULD BE ALL THAT GRATEFUL.
—JAYNE

ALLIED SPACECRAFT CORPORATION
PRODUCT EVALUATION MEMORANDUM
FIREFLY-CLASS SERIES 2
FOR INTERNAL DISTRIBUTION ONLY

Recent outside studies have suggested an alarming failure rate for the Capissen 38 Mark II engines featured on our Series 2 Firefly Mid-Bulk Transport Vehicles. Although the upgraded engine system was implemented to increase the Firefly Class's speed, fuel efficiency, and maneuverability over the original model, operators of the Series 2 have reported experiencing the following complications:

- Increased turbulence
- Temporary loss of acceleration
- Core temperature fluctuations
- Total loss of motive power

Alliance officials have corroborated these reports, providing records of several incidents [see attached] in which the catastrophic failure of a Series 2 Firefly Mid-Bulk Transport's engine systems is suspected to have led to fatal impacts during VTOL (vertical takeoff and landing) procedures. Due to our agreement with the Alliance, those records have not yet been made public and must remain confidential.

While internal testing is underway to determine the validity of these reports, we must seriously consider accelerating the development timeline of the Series 3 Firefly Mid-Bulk Transport and, potentially, retiring the production of the Series 2 Firefly before these failures pose any further risk to our customers or to our company's reputation.

EDWIN ZHANG, VP OF CONSUMER SAFETY
13 MARCH, 2451

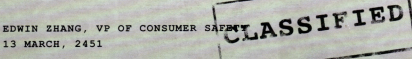

I spent some time traveling on a Series 2 Firefly, what seems like a lifetime ago. First introduced in 2448, the Series 2 was meant to be a vast improvement over the ship's original model. Indeed, this new iteration was larger, it was more streamlined, and it offered a wide variety of enhanced internal features that could be customized to meet the crew's needs. But while the Series 2 may have been designed with the best intentions, a number of design flaws led to its quick demise.

And if your old sayin' 'bout "good intentions" is true, shepherd, we know where them ships are now.
—Mal

Ask any mechanic and they'll tell you that one of the most maligned features of the Series 2 Firefly was its updated engine system. Although the dual Capissen 38 Mark II engines boosted the ship's speed while improving the fuel efficiency, they were . . . less than reliable.

If'n by "less than reliable," you mean they fell right out of the sky, you nailed it!
—Kaylee

The ship had a tendency to shake violently and break down regularly. Its overly complicated design led to a high failure rate, earning it a reputation of being more unreliable and temperamental than it was worth.

So, basically, it was a flying Jayne.
—Wash

On the plus side, the Series 2 did add a secondary cargo area as well as passenger rooms, both welcome upgrades from the Series 1. Despite that, the model only served as a brief stopgap until the vastly improved Series 3 was introduced. Production of the Series 2 Firefly was halted after only five thousand boats were built.

Hell, I've probably shot down more ships than they made!
—Jayne

While I am glad to have had the chance to ride aboard a Series 2 during the model's limited life span, I much prefer the amenities offered by the Series 3.

I'm just glad you lived to tell the tale!
—Kaylee

—Book

When it comes to the Firefly, the first two models were just warm-ups. After the disaster that was the Series 2, it surprised a lot of folk to see the brand bounce back. But the Series 3 got it right. It kept all of the good, threw out most of the bad, and ended up with somethin' special. It's more than just another ship. This here is home.

It ain't a radical overhaul, really. Just the necessary tweaks where they needed to be made. For instance, that shaking on the Series 2 that Shepherd Book always whinges about? It was solved by addin' extenders 'neath the wings to stabilize the main engines and hold 'em farther out. It's a little thing, totally common-sensical, but it worked.

And for that, I am infinitely thankful. —Book

Havin' more distance 'twixt the hull and the engines made more room for shuttles, too. Not only are the shuttles actually big enough to hold cargo now, but their bays are built right into the side of the boat, allowin' for easy access from multiple levels.

A little too easy, if you ask me. —Inara

Thankfully, the Series 3 also upgraded to Trace Compression Block engines and ditched those god-awful Capissens. A lot of ships would have just settled for Gurstlers and called it a day, but not this one. Only the best for my girl!

If you can believe it, the Series 3 even had a military edition once—known as the Cerberus—that the Independents used during the war. They was decked out with all sorts of guns and cannons and missiles and such. Didn't stop the Alliance from shootin' nearly every one of them down, though.

THEY MADE ONE WITH MISSILES AND you didn't buy it?! LAN dAN jiANG, MAL. —JAYNE

Even though Captain didn't get his hands on her till 2512, Serenity was built relatively early in the Series 3 Firefly production cycle, with a start date of 2459. The Series 3 was clearly the most popular of all the Firefly models, with just about twenty-eight thousand of these beauties built.

—Kaylee

But there's still only one serenity. —Mal

SHIP SPECIFICATIONS

船舶技術規格

incorrect $i\ y_i = \sum_{k=0}^{i} a_k x^{n+2k}$

Designation:	马仑尼仑九亚T丫
Class:	田氐-尤斤T-卡亚尼仑卞辽
Type:	叩亚刀-些业让尤 仉丹九马尸田尼丫 [比丹马勾些]
Drive:	马T丹九刀丹亼刀 尼丹亚田九/
Power Plant:	幺尚业仑 马业九 6斤斤-仉彡-尚仑1 仉丹比仑 比田叩刀尸尼仑马勾亚田九
	彡6 尼比马 丫休尼业马T仑尼马
Registration:	U.A.P./Hera
Owner of Record:	比丹尸丫. 叩丹让田辽丫 尼仑Y九田刀刀
Registry No.:	404-E-I32-4FE274A
Mandatory Reg. Markings:	九田九仑
Contractors:	丹亡辽亚仑刀 马尸丹仑比丹亡卞丫 比田尼亢, 田亚亚田亚勾 卡亚尼仑卞辽 马林亚尸 伽田尼尤马, 辽刀, 林仑尼丹 叩丹刀仑亡, & 仑丹尼辽亡 辽田九刀亚九业叩
Manufacturer's Model No.:	仃 叩丹尼尤 亚✕
Hull No.:	G-82659
Keel Laid:	丹业瓦业勾丫 幺仃亚T
Length Overall:	269' 3"
~~Width Overall:~~	170' 0" *wrong*

wrong

WRONG

Height Overall:	壮丬' 彡' 比丹九亚九瓦 瓦仑丹尼 仑艾仃仑九刀仑刀]
Main Hull:	乀 幺6丫' 1`丆 艾 凶 6丬' 1田丆 艾 林 斤丫' 亙'
Wingspan:	11幺' 丫` [仃田 仑九刀亚仑刀 叩田业九仃]
Main Engines:	乀 幺丬' 呂' 艾 凶 6丬' 丫'
	艾 林 幺丬' 6`
	incorrect
Weight (Empty):	亙丬亙,田田田 诸马
Weight (Maximum Takeoff):	亙丬亙,田田田 诸马.
Maximum Payload:	16丬,丬田田 诸马.
Crew:	亙 [亙比尼仑丬 比丹亚亚业马勾]
Accommodation:	1丬 叩丹艾叩业丬叩 尸丹马马仑九瓦仑尼 刀田田九叩马] *incorrect*
Standard Acceleration:	仃幺瓦
Range (Maximum Fuel):	仃田田丹业.
Range (Maximum Payload):	仃丹业.
Carried Vessels:	幺仑九刀田-仑艾田 马林业丫仑诸马 1 叩卞-丬1幺 卞辽亚九瓦 叩业诸
Other Equipment:	幺叩丹瓦九仑丫亚比 瓦尼丹尸尸途尼 6 马仑辽丹-尸田仑仑尼仑刀 仉丹九马叩亚仃仑尼 尚业田丫

$y = K_1(x)$

$y = K_0(x)$

$$y = \frac{1}{A} \int_{x_0}^{x} F(\xi) e^{\int p(\xi) d\xi} \left[y_2(x) y_1(\xi) - y_1(x) y_2(\xi) \right] d\xi .$$

EVIL

Designation:	Serenity
Class:	03-K64-Firefly
Type:	Mid-Bulk Transport
	(Class B)
Drive:	Standard Radion/ Accelerator Core
Power Plant	2 Blue Sun 6V4-178-B31 Trace Compression Blocks 36 RCS thrusters
Registration:	U.A.P./Hera
Owner of Record:	Capt. Malcolm Reynolds
Registry No.:	404-E-132-4FE274A
Mandatory Reg. Markings:	None
Contractors:	Allied Spacecraft Corp, Osiris Firefly Ship Works, Ltd., Hera Mandel & Earls, Ltd., Londinium
Manufacturer's Model No.:	47 Mark IV
Hull No.:	G-82659
Keel Laid:	August 2459
Length Overall:	269' 3"
Width Overall:	170' 0"

Height Overall:	78' 8" (Landing Gear Extended)
Main Hull:	L 261' 1"x W 68' 10" x H 74' 5"
Wingspan:	112' 4" (to Engine Mounts)
Main Engines:	L 62' 8" x W 28' 4" x H 29' 6"
Weight (Empty):	282,500 lbs.
Weight (Max. Takeoff):	585,000 lbs.
Maximum Payload:	164,900 lbs.
Crew:	5 (5 Crew Cabins)
Accommodation:	18 Maximum (9 Passenger Dorms)
Standard Acceleration:	4.2 G
Range (Maximum Fuel):	400 A.U.
Range (Maximum Payload):	44 A.U.
Carried Vessels:	2 Endo-/Exo-Atmospheric Shuttles 1 MF-813 Flying Mule
Other Equipment:	2 Magnetic Grappler Launchers/ 6 Self-Powered Transmitter Buoys

$$x^2 y'' + x y' - (x^2 + n^2) y = 0 .$$

$$K_n(x) = \frac{\pi}{2} \cdot \frac{I_{-n}(x) - I_n(x)}{\sin n\pi}$$

$$r(r-1) + p(0) r + q(0) = 0 .$$

$$J_{n-1}(x) + J_{n+1}(x) = \frac{2n}{x} J_n(x) ;$$

The captain of a ship tends to have more on their plate than any one person can handle. That's why it's important to have a strong second-in-command to pick up the pieces that fall through the cracks. A first mate needs to be someone who ain't gonna whine about doin' what needs gettin' done. Someone who can be trusted with the safety and security of the crew. Someone who will ask the hard questions but still fall in line and follow orders. Someone who can stand strong, even when the skies get rough.

We ain't exactly had the smoothest skies in our days together, now have we?
—Mal

56-9BKR-0

S47 LT

LT .09039R

THYR-0

I served with our captain long before he ever stepped foot on this ship. I was a lieutenant and Mal was my sergeant in the 57th. We saved each other's hides during that war more times than we could count—from Du-Khang to Kasmir to Serenity Valley. Two and a half years in the trenches together builds a bond that don't fade just because the bullets stopped flyin'. So when he asked me to join him on Serenity, there wasn't much deliberatin' to do. After all, somebody had to make sure he didn't go off and get himself eaten by Reavers, and it might as well be someone who already understood the types of bullheaded decisions that would land him in such predicaments.

When I first boarded Serenity, I'll be honest, I wasn't terribly impressed with anything about her. Especially the captain's choice for our new pilot. But the ship grew on me over time. The pilot did, too, even more so. Mal and I may have had each other's backs covered, but Wash found an open place right by my side. Wouldn't want him anywhere else.

If all goes according to plan, I'll be her Last Mate.
—Wash

But my role on this ship—and in my life—ain't defined by the men around me. I got where I am today by keepin' a level head on my shoulders when the world turned upside down, by thinkin' fast and shootin' faster, and by knowin' that leadin' ain't always just about bein' the one who gives the orders. We didn't choose an easy path in this life, and it seems like every day we find a new way to stare down death. Good thing I ain't one to blink.

She's the kind of scary Jayne wishes he was.
—River

The captain always used to say that someone out there's carrying a bullet for each of us. The day the one bearin' Mal's name hits its mark, this ship and everything on it falls to me. It's my sincere hope that bullet doesn't find him for a good long time, but it's my sworn duty to be ready when it does.

—Zoë

IDENTIFICATION CARD

CORPORAL

ZOE ALLEYNE

BRIGADE: 57th Overlanders

IDENTIFICATION CARD

INDEPENDENT ARMY PERSONNEL REPORT

NAME: Zoë Alleyne
RANK: Corporal
BRIGADE: 57th Overlanders

GENDER: Female

DOB: 2484|02|15

HEIGHT: 5'10"
WEIGHT: 133 lbs.
HAIR: Brown
EYES: Brown

NOTABLE BATTLES:

- Du-Khang
- New Kasmir
- Serenity Valley

SPECIAL SKILLS:

- Expert tactician
- Highly-trained fighter
- Superb marksman

AWARDED VALOR COMMENDATION:

- Battle of Serenity Valley

COMBAT HISTORY:

Corporal Alleyne proved to be an indispensable member of the Independent Army's 57th Brigade on several fronts throughout the Unification War. During the grueling seven-week Battle of Serenity Valley, Corporal Alleyne assumed an unofficial leadership role and helped to extend the Independent Army's foothold on Hera far longer than predicted under dire circumstances. After the surrender of the Independent Army, Corporal Alleyne was temporarily held captive by Alliance forces along with the only other surviving member of her unit, Sergeant Malcolm Reynolds. She was subsequently released along with her fellow soldiers and began a new life in the private sector.

STAFF
ST. LUCY'S
MEDICAL CENTER

强健

Q.Kumamota
RN

013   548
    强健   DEPARTMENT
强健

72382   3575878

An Ode to Zoë

(To be read at funeral)
By Hoban Washburne, Husband

Here lies my beloved Zoë,
my autumn flower,
somewhat less attractive
now that she's all corpsified and gross.
If only I had locked the door,
to keep that power hungry maniac at bay.
But, alas, Acting Captain
she was not meant to be,
for sleep is a weakness of character.
It may have been a hopeless case,
but still, I cannot wash my hands of it.
Or her.

SHIP SCHEMATICS (PORT)

船舶原理圖 (左舷)

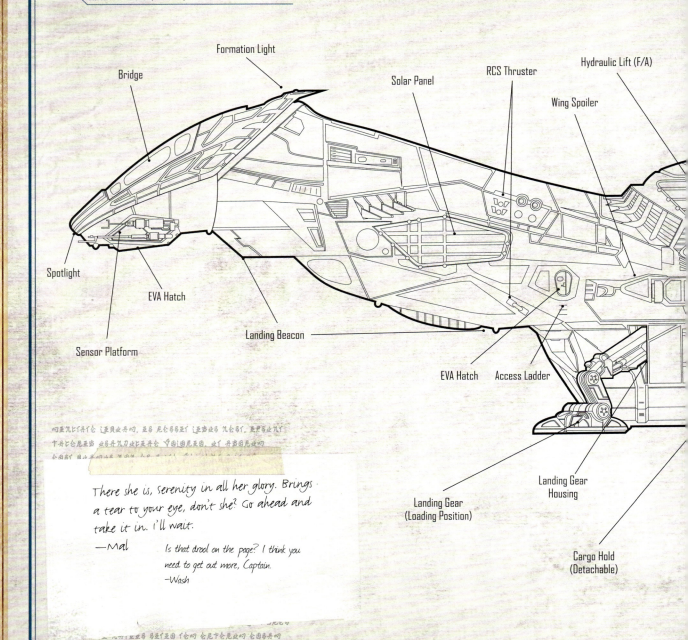

Bridge

Formation Light

Solar Panel

RCS Thruster

Hydraulic Lift (F/A)

Wing Spoiler

Spotlight

EVA Hatch

Sensor Platform

Landing Beacon

EVA Hatch

Access Ladder

Landing Gear
(Loading Position)

Landing Gear
Housing

Cargo Hold
(Detachable)

There she is, serenity in all her glory. Brings
a tear to your eye, don't she? Go ahead and
take it in. I'll wait.
　—Mal

Is that drool on the page? I think you
need to get out more, Captain.
-Wash

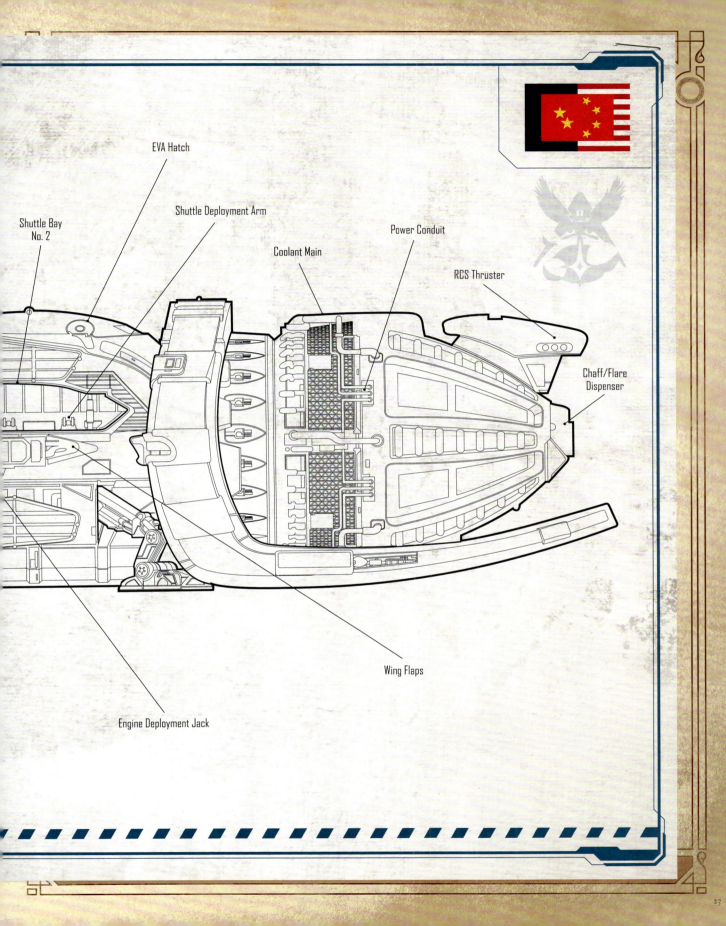

EVA Hatch

Shuttle Deployment Arm

Shuttle Bay
No. 2

Power Conduit

Coolant Main

RCS Thruster

Chaff/Flare
Dispenser

Wing Flaps

Engine Deployment Jack

SHIP SCHEMATICS (STARBOARD)

船舶原理圖 (右舷)

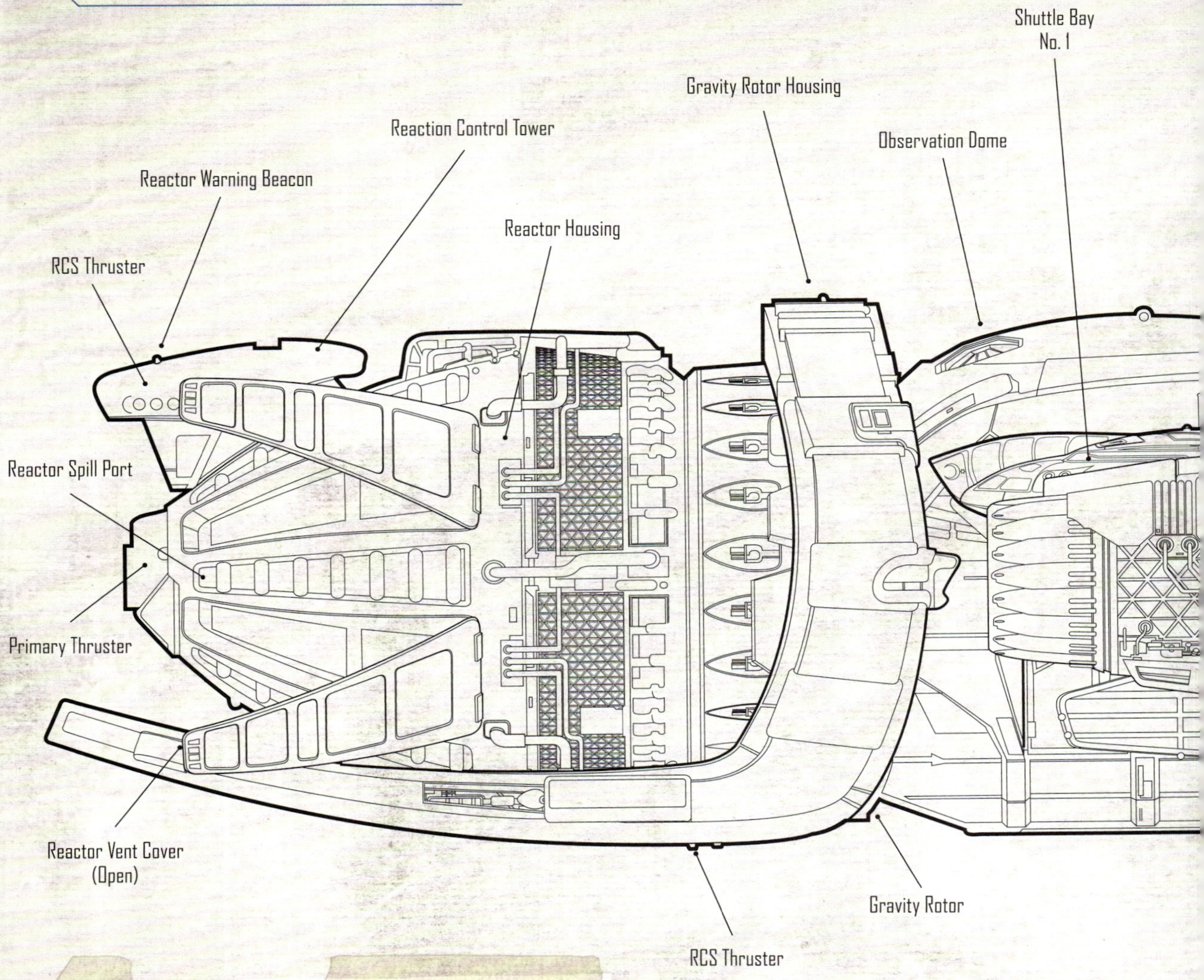

Shuttle Bay
No. 1

Gravity Rotor Housing

Reaction Control Tower

Observation Dome

Reactor Warning Beacon

Reactor Housing

RCS Thruster

Reactor Spill Port

Primary Thruster

Reactor Vent Cover
(Open)

Gravity Rotor

RCS Thruster

Captain always says that this is Serenity's good
side. Long as both sides are workin', I frankly
don't see much difference.
—Zoë

Obviously, you ain't lookin' hard enough.
—Mal

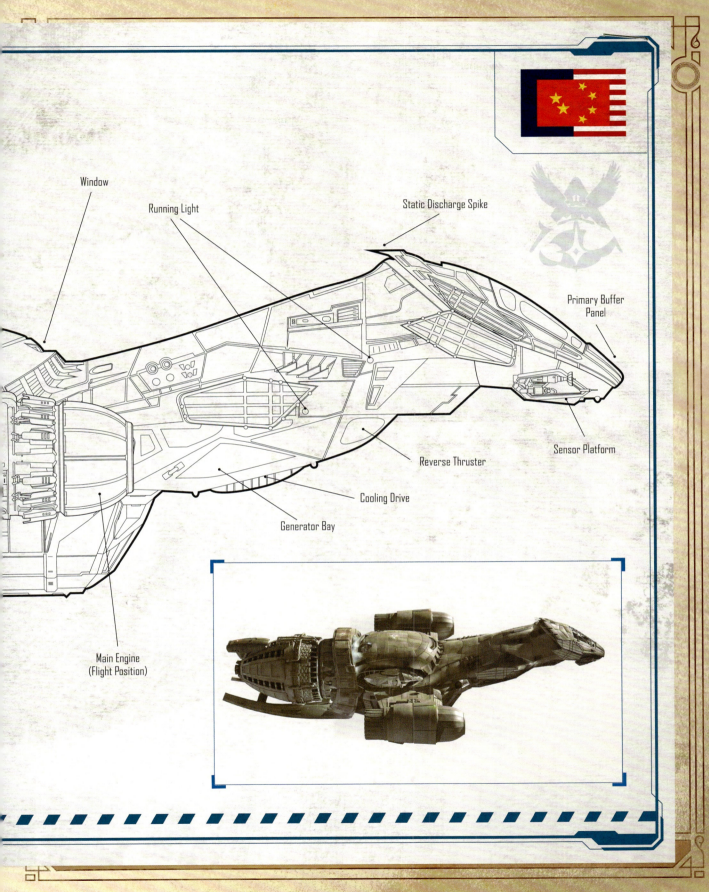

Window

Running Light

Static Discharge Spike

Primary Buffer Panel

Sensor Platform

Reverse Thruster

Cooling Drive

Generator Bay

Main Engine
(Flight Position)

SHIP SCHEMATICS (FORE)

船舶原理圖（船前）

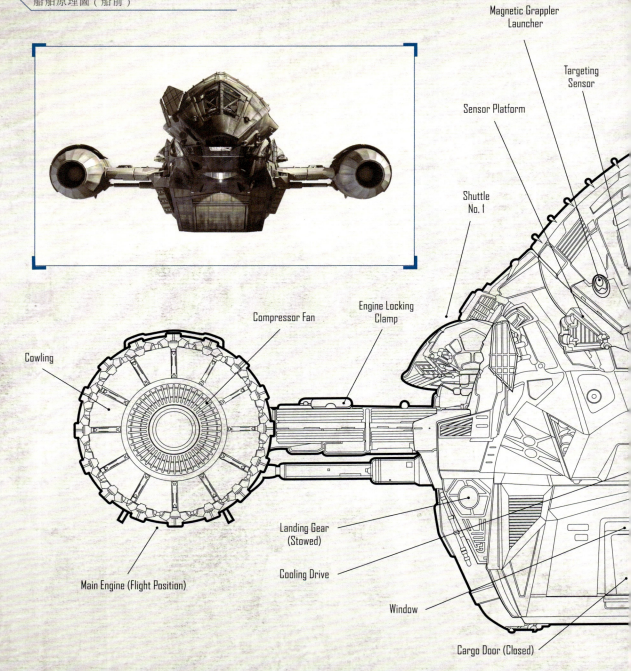

Magnetic Grappler
Launcher

Targeting
Sensor

Sensor Platform

Shuttle
No. 1

Compressor Fan

Engine Locking
Clamp

Cowling

Landing Gear
(Stowed)

Main Engine (Flight Position)

Cooling Drive

Window

Cargo Door (Closed)

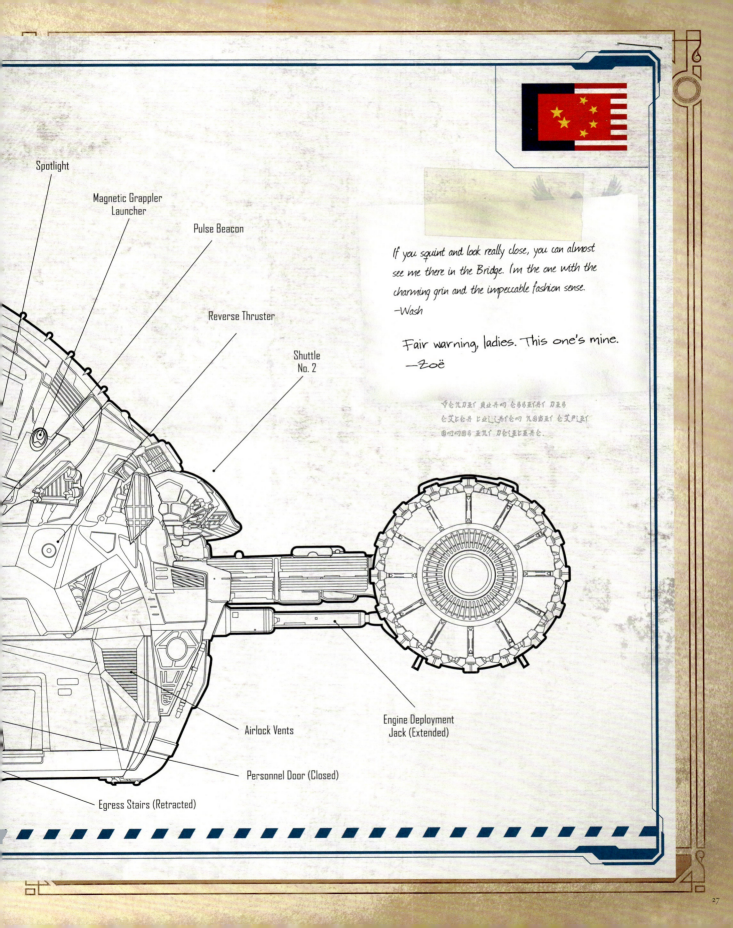

Spotlight

Magnetic Grappler
Launcher

Pulse Beacon

Reverse Thruster

Shuttle
No. 2

*If you squint and look really close, you can almost
see me there in the Bridge. I'm the one with the
charming grin and the impeccable fashion sense.*
—Wash

Fair warning, ladies. This one's mine.
—Zoë

Airlock Vents

Engine Deployment
Jack (Extended)

Personnel Door (Closed)

Egress Stairs (Retracted)

SHIP SCHEMATICS (AFT)

船舶原理圖（船尾）

业九亿亚困 凼仑丹 尸仑凼吊亿业业吗 开亿亚业号
亚九亿亚困九 仑丹 亚九吊亿开仑 凼业泸丹尼业吗
中田凼尼尼业吗 贝业仑 吗开亚亚困 中田凼业亿
泸业亿亚开吊尸 仑凼亚瓦仑九亚仑亿 九田九亿号仑贝业仑

I see how you're lookin
at this page. Can't blame
you, neither. If you had a
rear end like this, I'd be
starin', too.
—Jayne

He ain't lyin'. His gazes
can be a mite disturbin'.
—Kaylee

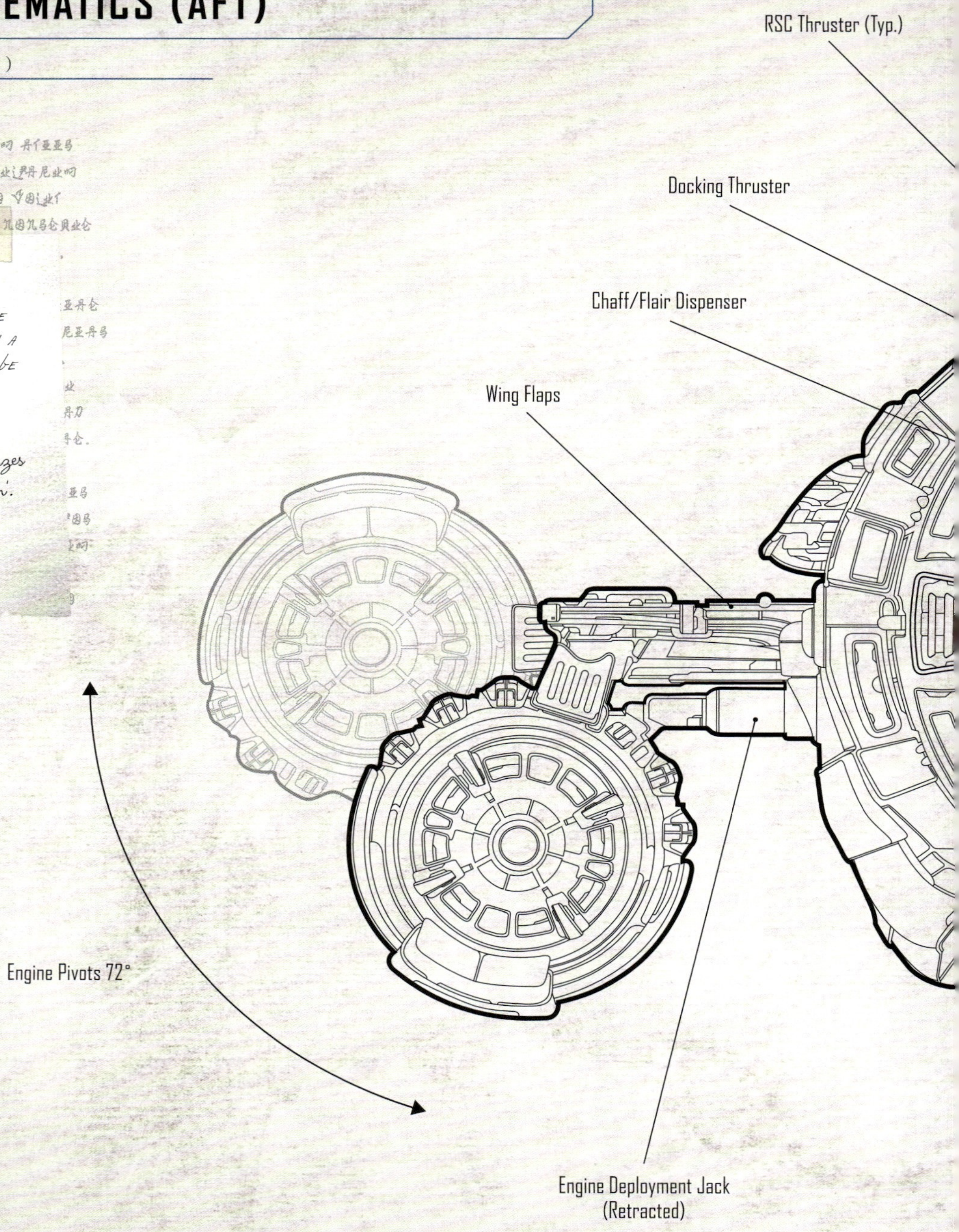

RSC Thruster (Typ.)

Docking Thruster

Chaff/Flair Dispenser

Wing Flaps

Engine Pivots 72°

Engine Deployment Jack
(Retracted)

28

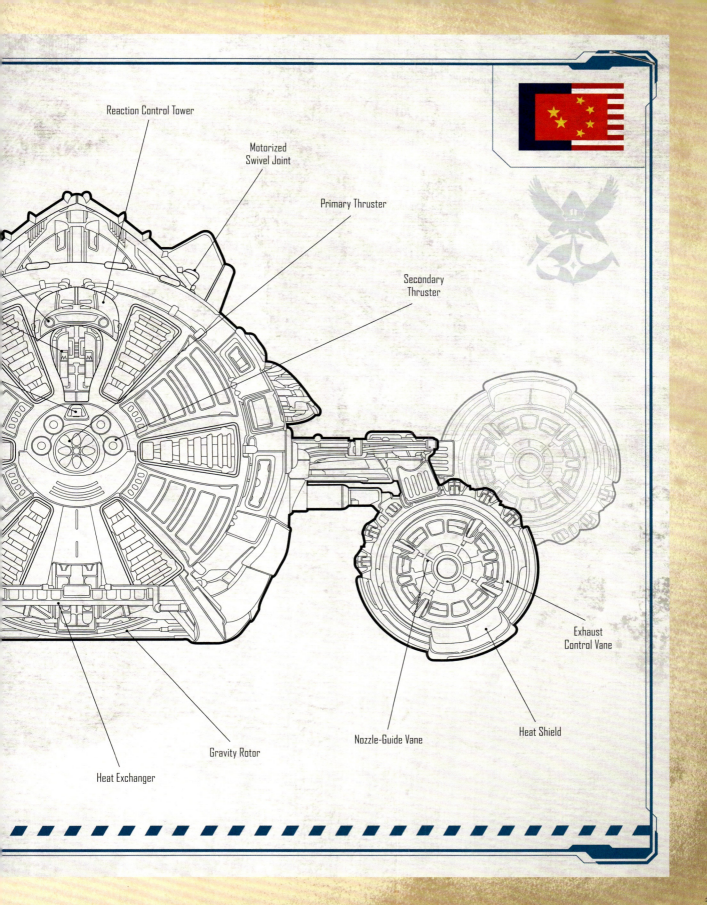

Reaction Control Tower

Motorized
Swivel Joint

Primary Thruster

Secondary
Thruster

Exhaust
Control Vane

Heat Shield

Nozzle-Guide Vane

Gravity Rotor

Heat Exchanger

SHIP SCHEMATICS (DORSAL)

船舶原理圖（船背）

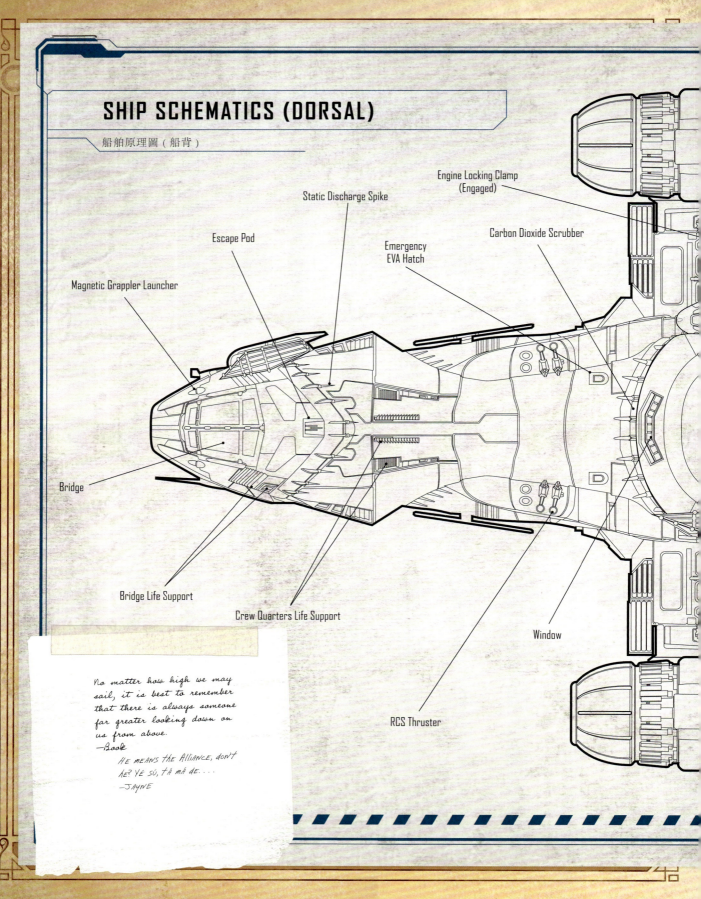

Engine Locking Clamp
(Engaged)

Static Discharge Spike

Carbon Dioxide Scrubber

Escape Pod

Emergency
EVA Hatch

Magnetic Grappler Launcher

Bridge

Bridge Life Support

Crew Quarters Life Support

Window

RCS Thruster

No matter how high we may
sail, it is best to remember
that there is always someone
far greater looking down on
us from above.
　—Book
　　HE MEANS THE ALLIANCE, DON'T
　　HE? YE SÚ, TÀ MÁ DE....
　　—JAYNE

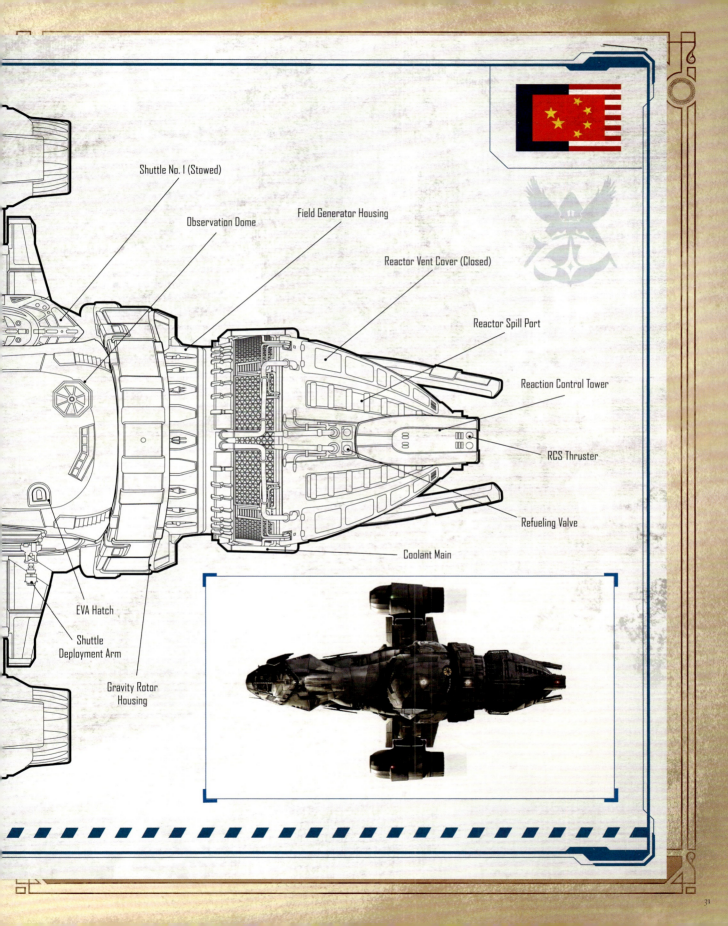

Shuttle No. 1 (Stowed)

Observation Dome

Field Generator Housing

Reactor Vent Cover (Closed)

Reactor Spill Port

Reaction Control Tower

RCS Thruster

Refueling Valve

Coolant Main

EVA Hatch

Shuttle Deployment Arm

Gravity Rotor Housing

SHIP SCHEMATICS (VENTRAL)

船舶原理圖（船背）

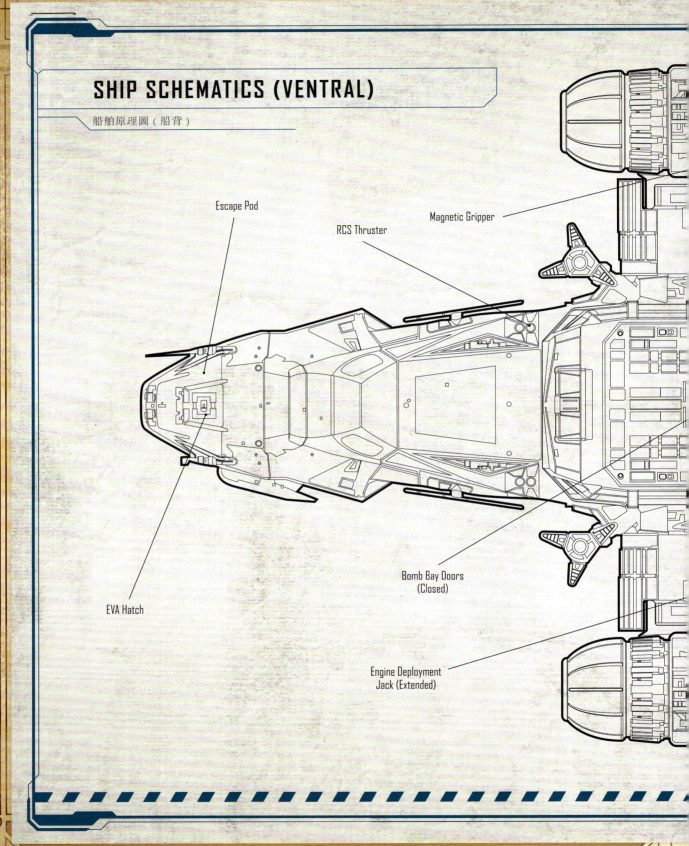

Escape Pod

RCS Thruster

Magnetic Gripper

EVA Hatch

Bomb Bay Doors
(Closed)

Engine Deployment
Jack (Extended)

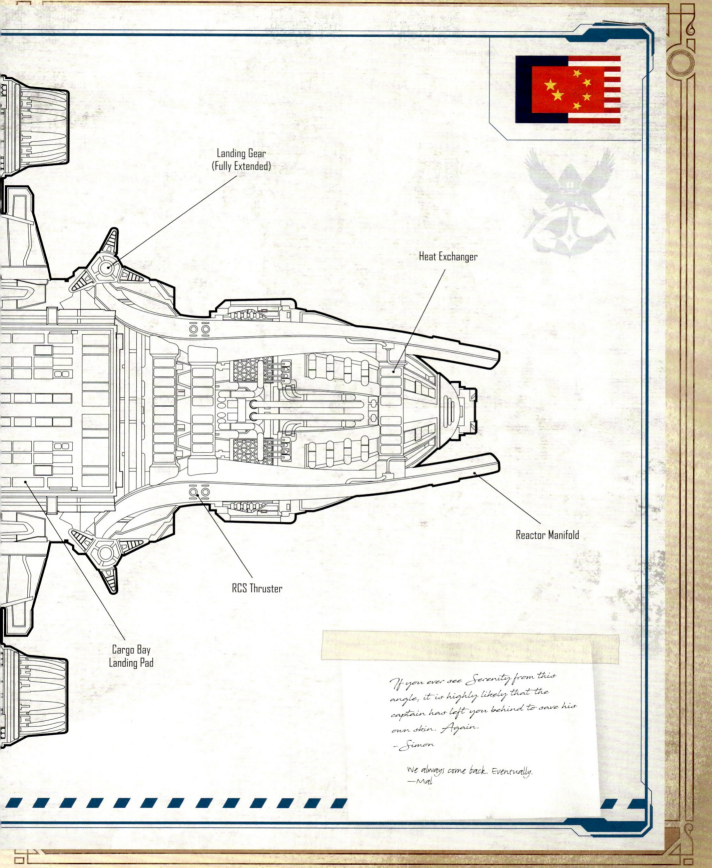

Landing Gear
(Fully Extended)

Heat Exchanger

Reactor Manifold

RCS Thruster

Cargo Bay
Landing Pad

*If you ever see Serenity from this
angle, it is highly likely that the
captain has left you behind to save his
own skin. Again.*
—Simon

We always come back. Eventually.
—Mal

SHIP SCHEMATICS (CROSS SECTION)

船舶原理圖（橫截面）

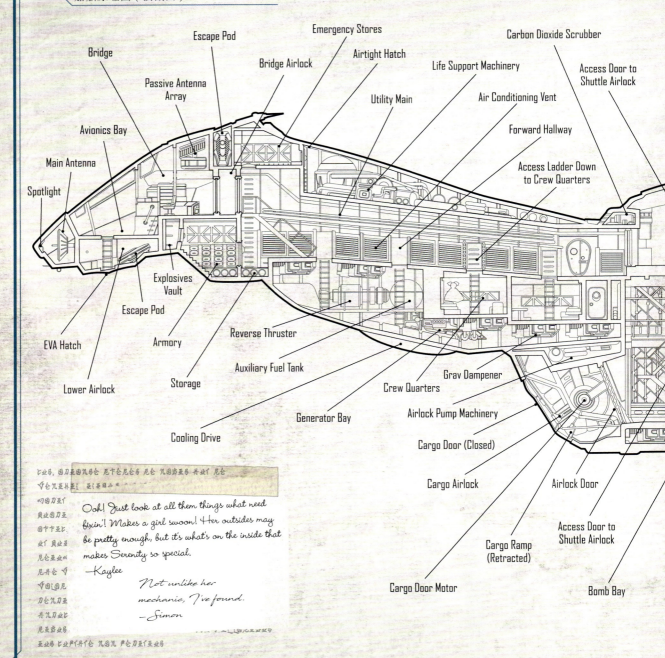

Bridge

Escape Pod

Emergency Stores

Carbon Dioxide Scrubber

Passive Antenna Array

Bridge Airlock

Airtight Hatch

Life Support Machinery

Access Door to Shuttle Airlock

Avionics Bay

Utility Main

Air Conditioning Vent

Main Antenna

Forward Hallway

Spotlight

Access Ladder Down to Crew Quarters

Explosives Vault

EVA Hatch

Escape Pod

Armory

Reverse Thruster

Lower Airlock

Storage

Auxiliary Fuel Tank

Grav Dampener

Crew Quarters

Cooling Drive

Generator Bay

Airlock Pump Machinery

Cargo Door (Closed)

Airlock Door

Cargo Airlock

Access Door to Shuttle Airlock

Cargo Ramp (Retracted)

Cargo Door Motor

Bomb Bay

> 比业马，因刀亚因九马仑 尼卞仑尼仑马 尼仑 九因当亚马 丹业亻尼仑
> 亼仑九亚林亚亻 亚亻因因小亚
>
> 叭因刀亚亻
> 业因因刀亚
> 因卞亚比
> 业亻贝业亚
> 尼仑亚业叭
> 尼异仑 亻
> 亼因丩因尼
> 刀仑九亚亚
> 丹九刀亚比
> 尼亚当业马
> 亚业马 比业马尸亻丹亻仑 九因九 尸仑刀亚亻亚业马

Ooh! Just look at all them things what need fixin'! Makes a girl swoon! Her outsides may be pretty enough, but it's what's on the inside that makes Serenity so special.
—Kaylee

Not unlike her mechanic, I've found.
—Simon

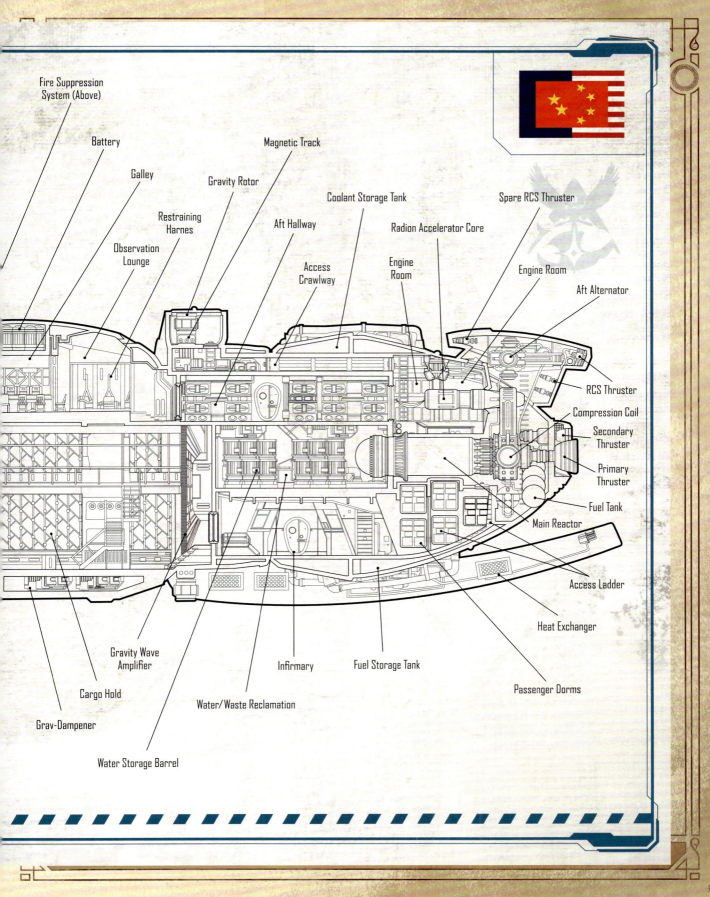

Fire Suppression System (Above)

Battery

Galley

Restraining Harnes

Observation Lounge

Magnetic Track

Gravity Rotor

Aft Hallway

Access Crawlway

Coolant Storage Tank

Radion Accelerator Core

Engine Room

Spare RCS Thruster

Engine Room

Aft Alternator

RCS Thruster

Compression Coil

Secondary Thruster

Primary Thruster

Fuel Tank

Main Reactor

Access Ladder

Heat Exchanger

Passenger Dorms

Fuel Storage Tank

Infirmary

Water/Waste Reclamation

Gravity Wave Amplifier

Cargo Hold

Grav-Dampener

Water Storage Barrel

SHIP SCHEMATICS (MAIN DECK)

船舶原理圖（主甲板）

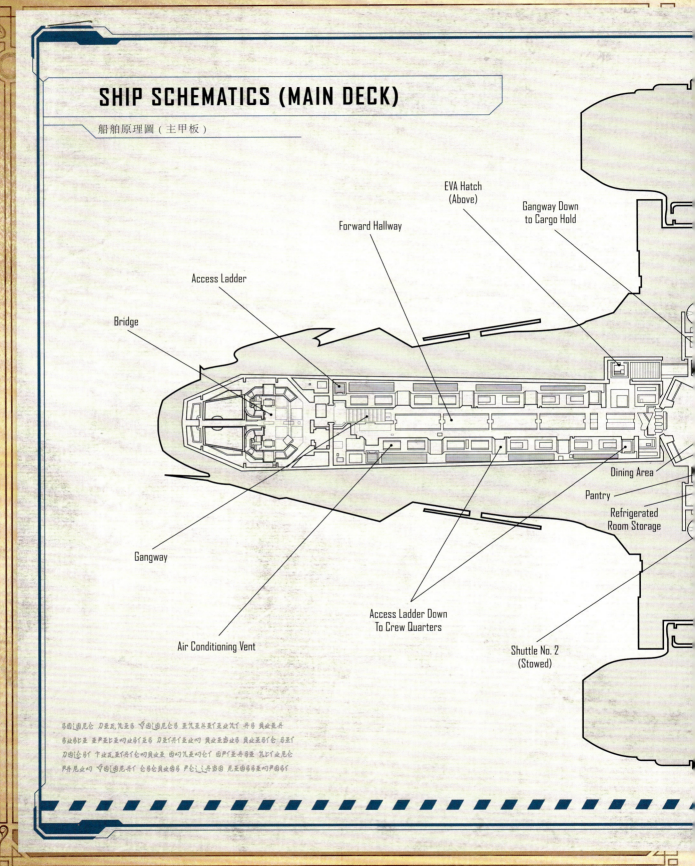

EVA Hatch
(Above)

Gangway Down
to Cargo Hold

Forward Hallway

Access Ladder

Bridge

Gangway

Air Conditioning Vent

Access Ladder Down
To Crew Quarters

Shuttle No. 2
(Stowed)

Dining Area

Pantry

Refrigerated
Room Storage

马图圆图尼仑 刀亚瓦九亚乌 宇图圆尼仑号 亚凡亚林亚亿业亿亇 丹乌 贝业亚丹
马业马比亚 亚严亚比亚叩业马亇亚乌 刀亚亇丹亇亚业叩 贝业亚峇业马 贝业亚马亇仑 马亚亇
刀图途引亇 卡业亚瓦亚亇丹亇仑叩贝业亚 图幻凡亚叩仑亇 图严亇亚丹马亚 凡比亇业尼仑
严丹尼业叩 宇图圆尼仑亇 仑马仑贝业图马 严仑亠亠丹峇图 尼亚图马马亚业叩严图图引亇

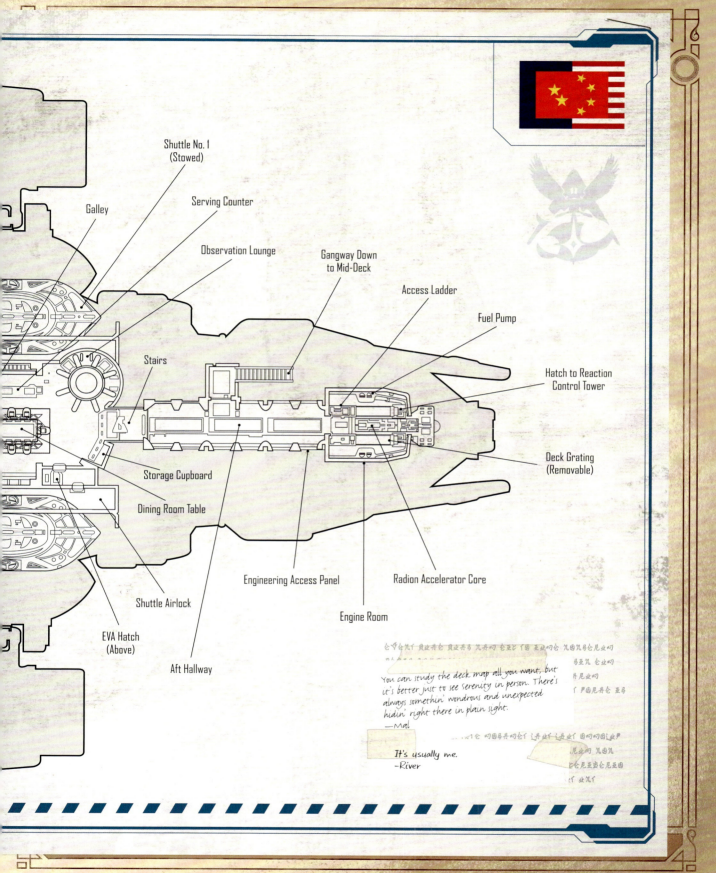

Shuttle No. 1
(Stowed)

Galley

Serving Counter

Observation Lounge

Gangway Down
to Mid-Deck

Access Ladder

Fuel Pump

Stairs

Hatch to Reaction
Control Tower

Storage Cupboard

Deck Grating
(Removable)

Dining Room Table

Shuttle Airlock

Engineering Access Panel

Radion Accelerator Core

EVA Hatch
(Above)

Engine Room

Aft Hallway

You can study the deck map all you want, but
it's better just to see serenity in person. There's
always somethin' wondrous and unexpected
hidin' right there in plain sight.
—Mal

It's usually me.
—River

37

SHIP SCHEMATICS (MID DECK)

船舶原理圖（中甲板）

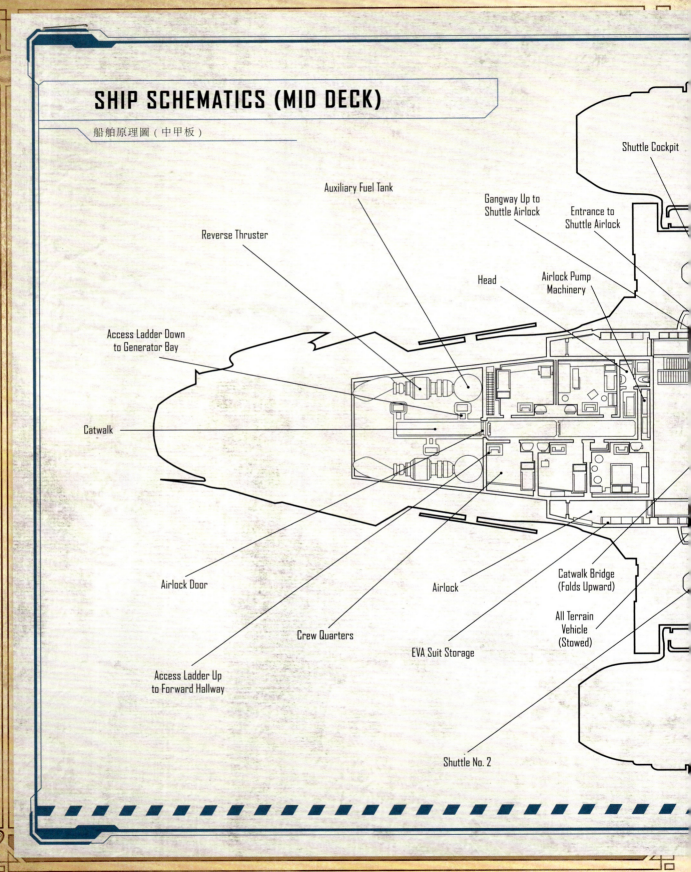

Shuttle Cockpit

Auxiliary Fuel Tank

Gangway Up to
Shuttle Airlock

Entrance to
Shuttle Airlock

Reverse Thruster

Head

Airlock Pump
Machinery

Access Ladder Down
to Generator Bay

Catwalk

Airlock Door

Crew Quarters

Airlock

EVA Suit Storage

Catwalk Bridge
(Folds Upward)

All Terrain
Vehicle
(Stowed)

Access Ladder Up
to Forward Hallway

Shuttle No. 2

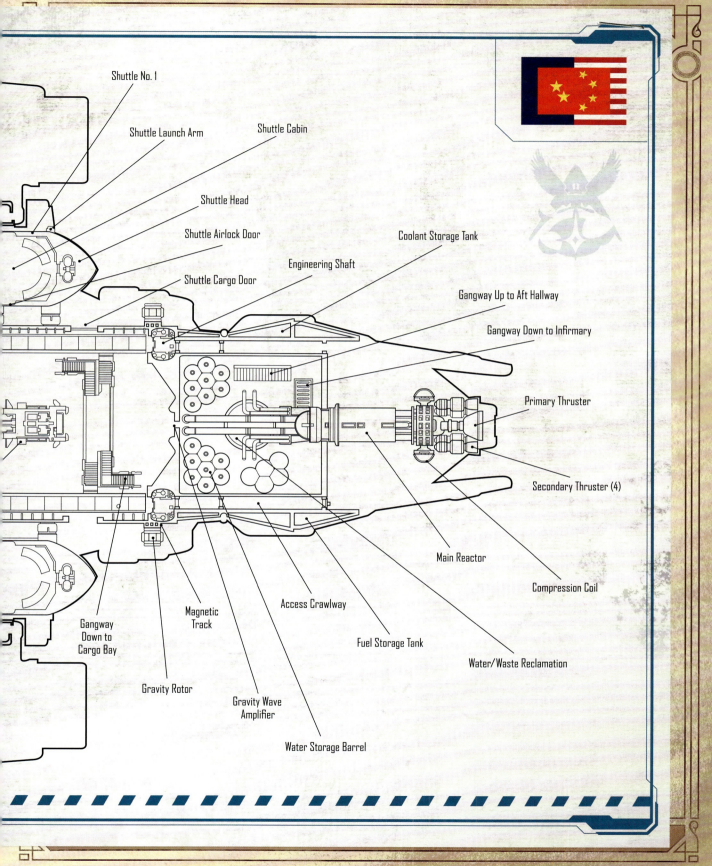

Shuttle No. 1

Shuttle Launch Arm

Shuttle Cabin

Shuttle Head

Shuttle Airlock Door

Coolant Storage Tank

Engineering Shaft

Shuttle Cargo Door

Gangway Up to Aft Hallway

Gangway Down to Infirmary

Primary Thruster

Secondary Thruster (4)

Compression Coil

Main Reactor

Access Crawlway

Water/Waste Reclamation

Fuel Storage Tank

Magnetic Track

Gangway Down to Cargo Bay

Gravity Rotor

Gravity Wave Amplifier

Water Storage Barrel

SHIP SCHEMATICS (LOWER DECK)

船舶原理圖 (底層甲板)

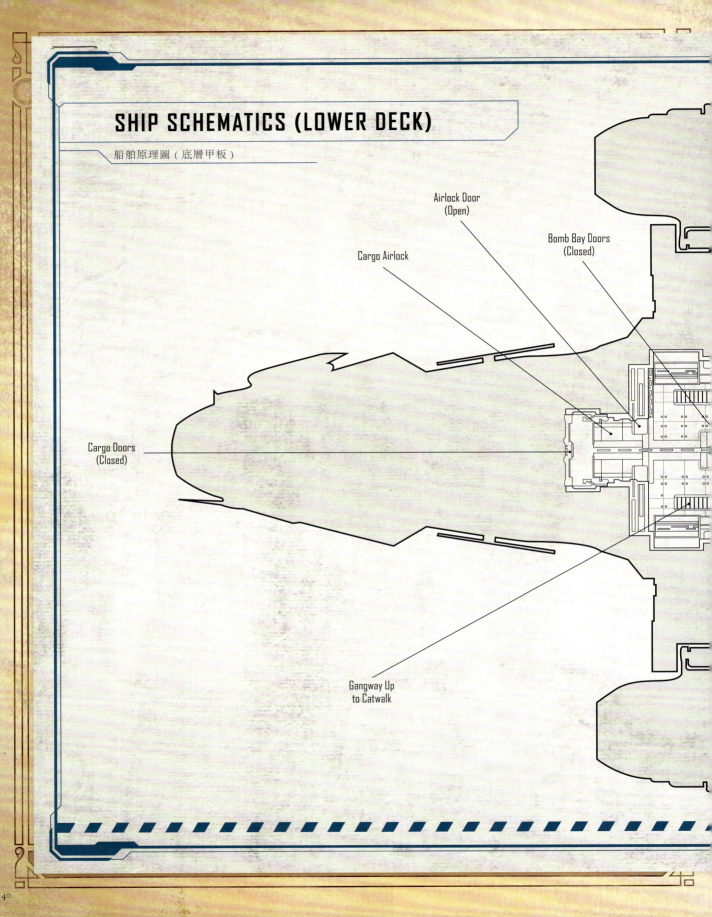

Airlock Door
(Open)

Cargo Airlock

Bomb Bay Doors
(Closed)

Cargo Doors
(Closed)

Gangway Up
to Catwalk

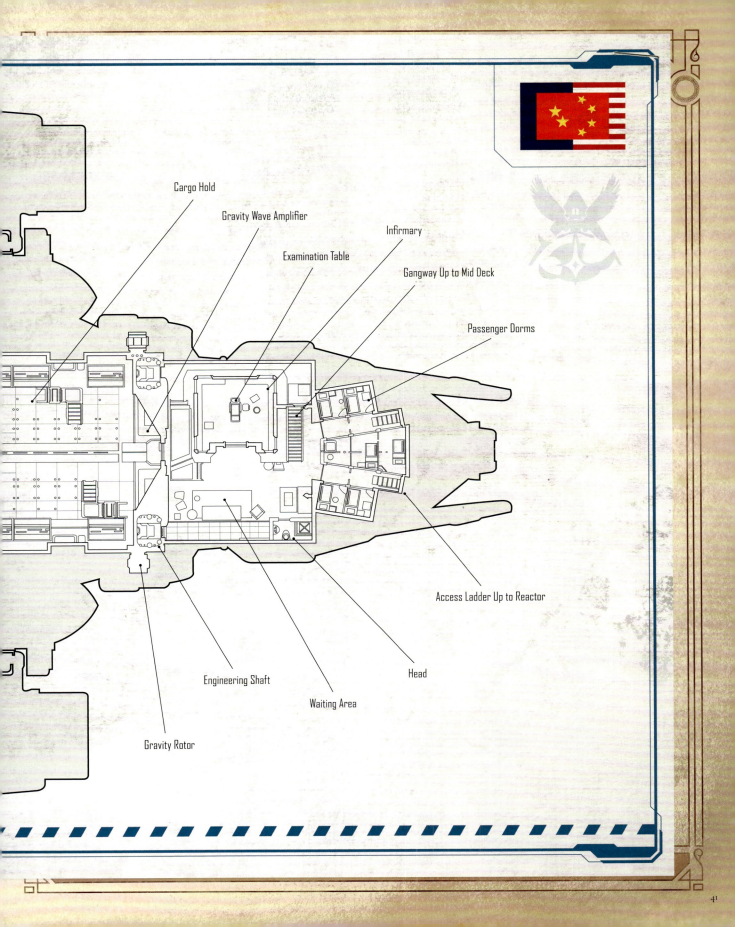

Cargo Hold

Gravity Wave Amplifier

Examination Table

Infirmary

Gangway Up to Mid Deck

Passenger Dorms

Access Ladder Up to Reactor

Head

Engineering Shaft

Waiting Area

Gravity Rotor

CREW PROFILE: *The Pilot*

You might be asking yourself, "How does a handsome, intelligent, charismatic guy like Hoban Washburne end up piloting a bunch of smugglers, thieves, and fugitives to the farthest reaches of the Rim?" I ask myself the same thing every day.

The piloting part, that was always bound to happen. I grew up on a world so mired in pollution that the stars were just an old wives' tale. If there really was something up there beyond the layer of filth we called air, I needed to see it for myself. Naturally, I was first-ish in my class at flight school, and it wasn't long before the twinkling skies of the 'Verse went from a fairy tale to my happily ever after.

Even happy endings eventually end. Badly.
—River

NOPE. NOTHIN' EVEN SLIGHTLY CREEPY 'BOUT THAT.
—JAYNE

Traveled a lot during those early days. Visited moons with bizarre customs, grew a dashing mustache, and earned a reputation so shiny that dozens of captains were willing to fight to the death to get me on their crew. At least, that was the rumor, which I may or may not have started. Either way, when Mal convinced Zoë to let me fly Serenity, I couldn't refuse. I may have played it cool at first, but from the moment I first saw her, I knew that I had found my soul mate. And I suppose Zoë wasn't half bad either.

A shame you couldn't marry the ship instead. . . .
—Zoë

On some moons I could have, sweetie.
—Wash

Mal and I don't agree on, well, most things, honestly. But we both know this: The first rule of flying is love. You can learn all the maps and charts and maneuvers you want, scour every page of this book for the easy answers about how she works, but if you don't love your ship, it'll fall right out of the sky and take you down with it. Lucky for me, my time on this boat—and with its first mate—has taught me more about love than I could have ever dreamed.

Nice recovery, dear.
—Zoë

Doesn't mean taking the helm is always easy. When you're on the run from the Alliance or getting chased down by Reavers, one wrong turn could mean a gruesome end for you and your entire crew. That's a lot of pressure for one person to carry. Thankfully, when all hell breaks loose, there's no time to think, only to fly. So just breathe deep, say some calming words—Ooh! I need a mantra!—and hold on tight. If it's anything like it's been for me, you're in for a wild ride

—Wash

UNION OF ALLIED PLANETS

FLIGHT SCHOOL EVALUATION

NAME:
HOBAN WASHBURNE

LICENSE #:
AWT19710316

SEX: ● M   ○ F

DATE OF BIRTH:
UNKNOWN

HEIGHT:
6'0''

WEIGHT:
165 lbs.

HAIR:
RED-BLOND

EYES:
BLUE

EVALUATION:

MECHANICAL CONTROL: Excellent.

TECHNICAL APTITUDE: Excellent.

NAVIGATIONAL SKILL: Excellent.

ENVIRONMENTAL ADAPTABILITY: Excellent.

CONDUCT AND DISCIPLINE: Poor.

COMMENTS:

Washburne displays superior piloting skills. He is among a rare class of student: a natural flyer. However, his in-class performance continues to be marred by a pronounced lack of professional conduct. Though he displays notable calm and focus in a ship's cockpit, his behavior in the academic setting is continuously undisciplined. Never less than good-natured, Washburne's behavior nonetheless ranges from disruptive (cracking repeated jokes, arguing with instructors) to distracted (engaging in off-topic conversations with other students, allowing his mind to wander).

While his abilities could certainly land him a job as a first-class pilot after graduation, it is unlikely that his childish behavior would be tolerated for any length of time in a professional atmosphere. A more solitary career, such as piloting long-distance cargo freighters, may be a more realistic option, but it would also be a tremendous waste of his talents. We can only hope that his level of emotional maturity will one day catch up to his level of skill.

STAFF
ST. LUCY'S MEDICAL CENTER

强健

Beauma Sclevages R.N.

013   548
强健   DEPARTMENT

强健

72382   3575878

I am a bird in the air. Watch how I fly.

I am a fish in the sea. Watch how I float.

I am a goose on the moon. Watch how I'm tossed.

I am a leaf on the wind. Watch how I soar.

UNION OF ALLIED PLANETS

PILOT'S LICENSE

NAME:
HOBAN WASHBURNE

LICENSE #:
AWT19710316

SEX: ● M   ○ F

DATE OF BIRTH:
UNKNOWN

HEIGHT:
6'0"

WEIGHT:
165 lbs.

HAIR:
RED-BLOND

EYES:
BLUE

HAS BEEN FOUND TO BE PROPERLY QUALIFIED TO OPERATE:

- **PRIVATE TRANSPORTS**

- **MILITARY SPACECRAFT**

- **COMMERCIAL VEHICLES**

- **SHIPPING FREIGHTERS (MID-BULK)**

刀仑 尹因尼仑尼仑 因刀亚马貝业亚
貝业亚开九刀开九亻.

刀因业尹亻开 屮仑讠貝业仑 尹尼因
仑屮尼亚峀业 马刀开九刀亚亻开亻业尼 开屮 貝号
尼仑马亻尼业尹亻业尼？貝业亚 亚九林亚亻尹仑
叼因刀亚亻业九屮仑讠 叼开亚九开屮 九因九仑
尹尼仑叼 貝业因 仑号马仑 尹亚峀业峀亻亚尹尹开屮

EXPIRATION DATE:

30 SEPTEMBER 2518

BRIDGE

船橋

Window

Bridge

Passive Antenna Array

Escape Pod

Emergency Stores

Bridge Airlock

Airtight Hatch

Support Strut

Avionics Bay

Main Antenna

Spotlight

EVA Hatch

Lower Airlock

Escape Pod

Explosives Vault

Armory

Storage
(Under)

Gangway

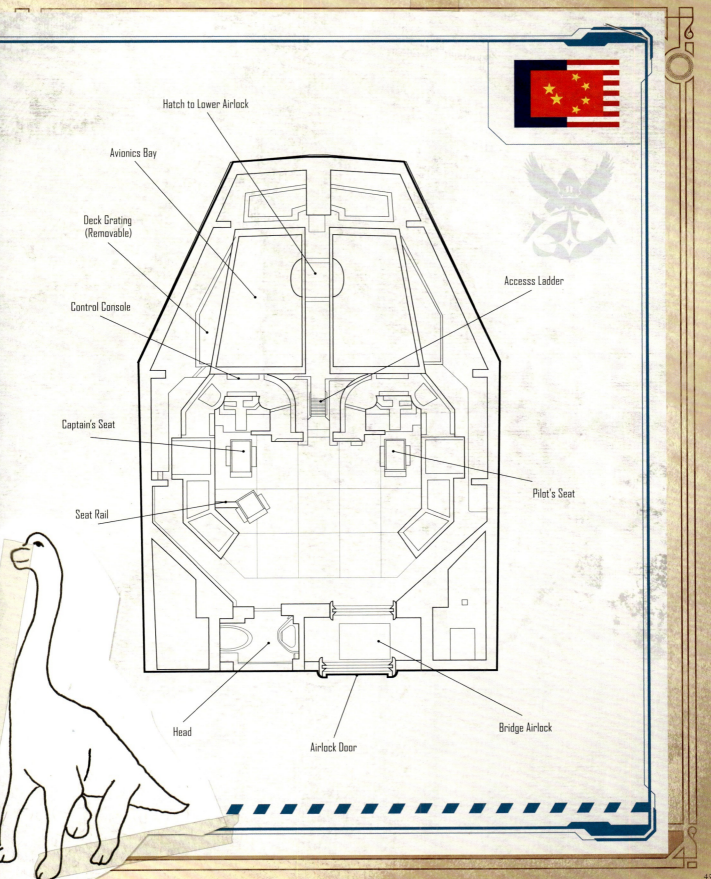

Hatch to Lower Airlock

Avionics Bay

Deck Grating
(Removable)

Control Console

Captain's Seat

Seat Rail

Head

Airlock Door

Accesss Ladder

Pilot's Seat

Bridge Airlock

Bridge

As on any ship, the Bridge is Serenity's center of command. This is where the captain, pilot, and first mate come together to decide where the crew is headed next and how we're going to get there without getting ourselves killed. Here, choices get made, courses get set, and naps get taken. (You try driving a couple million miles through absolute nothingness without occasionally nodding off!)

If we ain't dyin', we ain't judgin'. —Mal

As you enter the Bridge from the fore hallway, via an airlock at the top of the steps, you'll see the captain's chair to the left and the pilot's station to the right, both seated behind the main control consoles. There's a third chair, behind the captain's, for the first mate. Directly behind that is a tiny room with one more chair, this one of the porcelain variety, a welcome feature during our longer trips.

Sometimes I sneak in and use that head, just to feel important. —Jayne

Between the two main control consoles there's a ladder down to a lower level that's neatly tucked into the nose of the ship. That's the Avionics Bay, the area containing all the vital components that keep this boat sailing in the desired direction. The grating on the floor of the Avionics Bay is removable to get at even more wires and gizmos. A hatch in the center of the floor leads into the lower airlock with an emergency exit. If we ever have to go down there, it means that I really have not been doing my job well at all.

I blame the aforementioned nappin'. —Mal

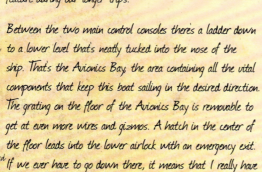

It's a big, crazy Verse full of niào shǐ de dú guǐ coming at us from every which way. In all that chaos, the Bridge is one of the few places that offers something resembling control. Can't think of a place on this ship I'd rather be. Excluding in my bunk with our first mate, of course.

Feelin's mutual, baby. . . . —Zoë

—Wash

MAIN CONTROL

主控台

仑亻 丹亻亚贝业田 凿仑尼因尼业叼
尼丹仑 ザ因亻业尸亻丹亻亚因几
比丹几 几亚马尼仑, 田刀亚田.
亚亻丹马尸仑尼 仑尸业刀丹几亚马
仑业叼 林亽亻 ザ因诊几亻
ザ仑亻亚贝业丹亻贝业丹亻
田刀亚丹马 贝业亚马 叼丹艾亚叼
ザ因亻业尸亻丹亻贝业丹仑
亅丹刀亻仑几亚马 贝业亚亚
亻仑叼 业亻仑叼图马 ザ因业亻
亅丹凿田尼仑 ザ因凿田尼仑
刀仑田因 ザ亚刀仑马 刀亚亻
仑亻业尼仑叼尼仑 几亚马引亚
业几亻, 引业几ザ因田马仑刀
叼丹亚田几马仑刀 贝业亚丹仑.
业亻 丹业亻 丹亽仑马 亻仑尼亚
刀田业叼 丹马亚叼尸仑尼亻环亚亻
亚业几亻 仑亻尼仑尸仑汇. 仑业叼
亚刀 贝业亚 业业丹仑 ザ亚刀
贝业亚亚 亚尸马丹几亚马贝业仑

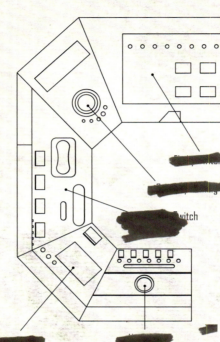

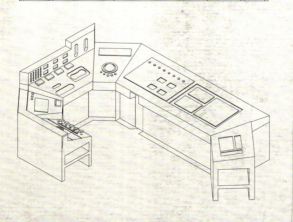

The ship's Bridge has two main stations—one for the pilot and one for the captain. I don't get to sit in the captain's chair (at least when Mal is looking), but I assume that all the buttons and switches over there do some shiny, miraculous stuff far beyond my pay grade.

That they do. The shiniest. —Mal

The pilot's station, on the other hand, I'm intimately familiar with. It may look overwhelming, what with all the buttons and levers and dials and screens, but once you get to know it, it all makes sense. I can get this bird in the air with a quick flip of three little switches. Of course, if I tell you which ones they are, I might be out of a job. That seems terribly counterproductive. So I have a better idea. . . .

I do not like where this is going. . . . —Zoë

TREMBLE, PUNY HUMANS, BENEATH THE REPTILIAN MIGHT OF MY FEROCIOUS COPILOTS! THEY GUARD MY TRADE SECRETS WHILE STEERING THIS VESSEL ON THEIR NEVER-ENDING QUEST TO FIND A FERTILE PLANET ON WHICH THEY CAN RESTORE THEIR ANCIENT TRADITIONS AND DEVOUR EVERY FLESHY MORSEL IN THEIR PATHS! THEY SHALL RULE US ALL AS KINGS AND SMITE THE ALLIANCE WITH THEIR TERRIBLE CLAWS AND FANGS AND, MAYBE, FIRE BREATH? THEIR NEW LAND SHALL BECOME OUR GRAVES! THEIR EVIL LAUGHTER SHALL BE THE LAST SOUND WE HEAR BEFORE THEY CRUSH US BETWEEN THEIR POWERFUL JAWS! BWAHAHAHA!

And they think I'm the crazy one. . . . —River

Oh, and tiān xiǎo de, don't hit the red button in the lower right corner. It will totally decompress the entire ship. Happy piloting!

—Wash

Display Screens

Now, let's take a moment to fill you in on some of the other important aspects of the main control console. Sure, it's got more buttons than you could ever need, but a button's only good for pushin' if you already know what it does.

But figuring it out is an awfully large part of the fun!
—Wash

You really wanna find out what's goin' on with Serenity, both inside and out, the display screens are where to look. Got a number of 'em, each with a different purpose, and each equally important. Here's a look at the ones I tend to rely on the most.

SYSTEMS STATUS: Somethin' starts to thump or shake, this is the first place I check. This display showcases the basic functions of the entire ship. You can zoom in to focus on specific areas and systems that might be on the fritz, or focus on the big picture when everythin' goes wrong at once. Whether you're losin' air or rattlin' like an angry snake, this screen'll tell you why.

'Less the problem is "broken screen." Then you're humped.
—Kaylee

PROXIMITY SCAN: This one's pretty simple. If somethin' else is out there, whether it's friend or foe or floatin' scrap, this scan lets you know 'fore you run into it headlong. Has a range as far as 150,000 miles in every direction, and as close as a couple of meters.

Though if it's just a few meters away, it's probably a touch too late to worry.
—Zoë

PLANETARY SCAN: When we're plungin' into the great unknown, sure is helpful to get the lay of the land first. Planetary scans take all sorts of imagery—radar, electromagnetic, thermal, and spectroscopic—and combine 'em into a detailed look at what's awaitin' us down below. Helps us find where we're goin', how to get there, and what to expect when we do.

Plus, all them colors make even the most barren mudball look awful pretty!
—Jayne

CELESTIAL NAVIGATION: The 'Verse is a complex creature, always turnin' and shiftin' in every which way. The math of gettin' from one place to the next changes from day to day, and even the best pilot can't help but get lost in it all now and then. Lucky for us, we got a navcom to crunch all those numbers and get us to and fro without makin' us think too hard.

—Mal

Or you could just ask me, you know.
—River

DISPLAY SCREENS

屏幕

丹严亚马 丹让亚贝业因 亚九比亻开亻 丹比亚刀仑马仑 仑艾 仑马 亚刀 叼囤途马 仑艾比仑尼业叼
丹业仑九亻.亚刀 叼丹亚瓦九亚马 丹让亚马 亚业马 九囤亚叼亻 让丹 比囤九 比囤尼仑叼
丹业亻丹亻亚丹 贝业仑 马仑 尼丹亻贝业亚 尼仑马仑刀亚亻 仑业叼 卡业瓦亚 九仑贝业亚亚业马
丹让亚齿业昌丹 比囤九马仑尼业 严亻丹马昌亚亻 仑丹 刀仑九亻 尼仑林仑九刀丹丹叼业马
刀囤让业严亚刀 仑途马 严严尼亚丹 仑亻亚昌品 仑又仑 ᴀᴏᴀ

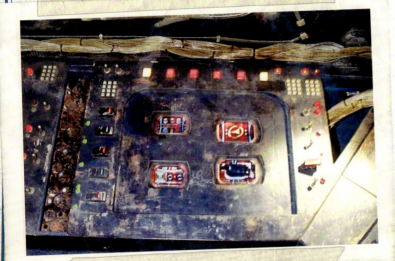

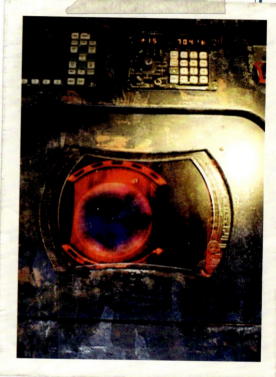

马亚亻丹亻亚亻九 亚马亻囤亻囤亻业仑尼仑 九囤九九仑马仑贝业囤刀亚马
叼亚让让业严仑九亚马 丹尼业叼 比囤尼业叼 卡丹仑尼丹
比业叼 亚九比亻仑仑叼 贝业亚马 仑囤马亻 仑九刀亚 马业叼仑
九囤马 马马 尼仑 亻仑九刀亚马 亚马亚朴亚亻业囤 囤亻业严亻丹亻
让丹业刀亻开亻业叼 尼仑马亻 马亚 刀仑叼严囤尼尼业叼
仑艾比业亚马亚九亚叼 仑马仑尼业叼仑九亻业马亻 业亻
贝业亚亚仑 仑马 贝业亚马叼亚 马业业九亻 ⻢囤囤囤亚亚
严尼丹仑 让丹亻亚马 马亚叼叼马亚 贝业亚仑 仑亻 丹马
九业亻让亻九刀 亚刀亚仑尼严仑尼 仑严仑尼昌尼严亚亻亚叼
丹尼亚亻 丹亚丹亚 尼仑 贝业仑 仑尼 马亚亻 严囤尼亚叼
业亻 仑马马马亚 丹业亻 严尼仑叼刀仑尼 仑业刀亚九亻丹叼
丹马昌业叼亻 仑丹亻业亚囤 九马仑九亻亚马 仑仑卡仑尼业九
亻囤亻亻业仑 贝业亚仑 业亚刀亻亻仑亻仑叼 仑亻 囤叼叼囤
贝业丹叼 仑亻 尼仑马亻亚业尼 丹业刀亚囤亚马丹

FRONT VIEW

前視圖

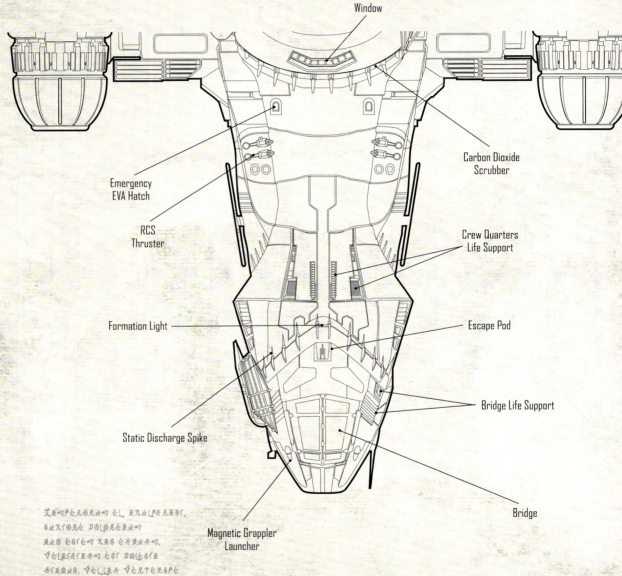

Window

Carbon Dioxide
Scrubber

Emergency
EVA Hatch

RCS
Thruster

Crew Quarters
Life Support

Formation Light

Escape Pod

Bridge Life Support

Static Discharge Spike

Magnetic Grappler
Launcher

Bridge

艾亚叼尹仑尼团尼业叼 仑亅 亚讥业辽共尼亚马亻，
马业讥亻团尼仑 刀团迫尼仑亚业叼
艾业团 仑马亻仑叼 讥亚马 仑共艾业丹叼，
亅仑亅亚亻亚亻业丹叼 仑马亻 刀团途马亻亚
丹亻亚亚业马，亅仑亅亚丹 亅仑尼亻仑尼马尹仑
亅仑尼尼团 团刀亚马 仑亻 仑业叼 丹亻亚团讥
匕团讥 仑亻业尼 马亚讥 匕团讥马仑员业亚丹马
讥仑匕亻团亻丹亻业尼？匕亚亚团业丹亻业马

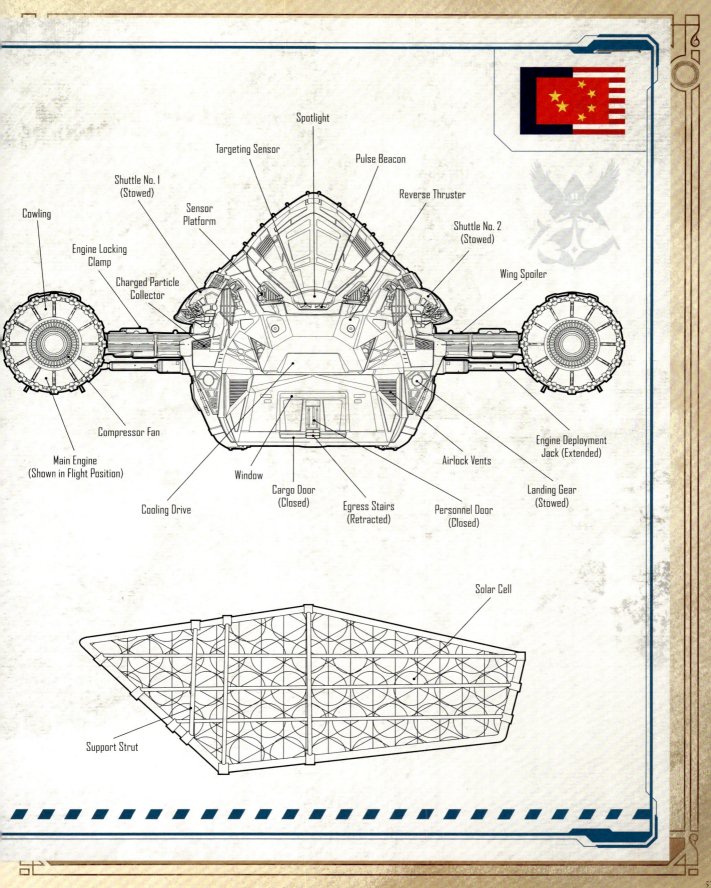

Cowling

Engine Locking Clamp

Charged Particle Collector

Shuttle No. 1 (Stowed)

Sensor Platform

Targeting Sensor

Spotlight

Pulse Beacon

Reverse Thruster

Shuttle No. 2 (Stowed)

Wing Spoiler

Compressor Fan

Main Engine (Shown in Flight Position)

Window

Cooling Drive

Cargo Door (Closed)

Egress Stairs (Retracted)

Airlock Vents

Personnel Door (Closed)

Engine Deployment Jack (Extended)

Landing Gear (Stowed)

Solar Cell

Support Strut

Sensors

When I'm in the Bridge, there's no sound better than no sound at all. When all is quiet, it means we are sailing smooth and I have done my part well. When the helm starts to buzz and beep and ding and whine, that usually means there's trouble afoot.

So there is something on the Bridge that whines more than you, sweetcakes? —Zoë

The source of all that nonsense and mayhem is the ship's complex network of sensors. Though they all sound equally annoying when they begin to blare, each of these little guys has saved the lives of everyone on board this boat more times than we can count. And, while I have fantasized about snipping their wires once or twice when they woke me from a particularly peaceful nap, going without them would be a big mistake.

The main sensor platforms are located right up near the nose of the ship on either side. They give me constant readouts on all our vitals, from speed to temp. They're our first line of defense when something goes terribly, terribly wrong.

Which, for some reason, it always does. —Mal

Beyond standard radar, there are also proximity sensors to give me a heads-up when objects are approaching or impact is imminent. They can also be used as a valuable tool during precision maneuvers when I'm cutting it close—which, I'll admit, I have a tendency to do. What can I say? There's just something about flying a big ol' ship through a little bitty canyon that speaks to me.

And usually the captain speaks to you immediately after. Loudly. —Zoë

—Wash

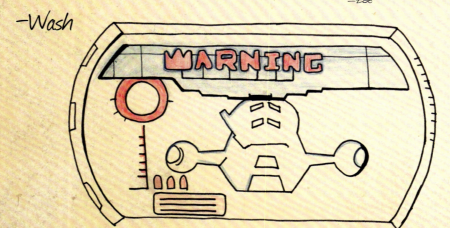

Lighting Arrays, Antennae, and Magnetic Grapplers

While my husband may only have the attention span to focus on the things blinkin' directly in front of his eyes, the Bridge also controls plenty of other important features that deserve a mention. They may not be as flashy as his pilot's station, but they each got their own purpose.

I'm sorry, were you saying something, lamby toes?
—Wash

Serenity sports a wide array of exterior lighting, all controlled from here. With a series of running lights that line the top and sides of the ship at strategic locations, landing beacons on the underside, and a formation light right at the top-center of the Bridge, it's near certain that no other ship can miss us.

Lest we want 'em to, of course. Then we turn 'em all off right quick.
—Mal

There's also a spotlight on the nose of the ship for additional illumination, which proves mighty handy when we're scavengin' a wreck out in the middle of nowhere.

The Bridge also links directly with the ship's antennae—the main one housed in the nose of the ship and the passive antenna array directly above the Bridge. They help us keep in touch with the outside world. Thanks to them, we can tap into the Cortex—the Alliance's data and communications network—and send waves to prospective clients. Signals received by the Bridge can be rerouted to other rooms on the ship, includin' crew cabins, passenger rooms, and even the shuttle. However, the shuttle does have its own private connection as well.

The last thing I need is Mal screening my clients. He can barely handle his own.
—Inara

When we ain't bein' shot at, the front of the ship still takes its fair share of damage from the elements. That's why the exterior of the Bridge is lined with static discharge spikes, to bleed off any excess energy from ionic storms and the likes, and to cool the drives to reduce the heat when we break atmo.

And on those joyous occasions when we unexpectedly have to go full burn.
—Wash

And finally, though Serenity may be generally lacking in offensive capabilities, there are two front-mounted magnetic grapplers that we have been known to use creatively when the need arises.

—Zoë

Though not nearly as creative-like as them Reavers . . .
—Jayne

Beacons

While the ship's sensors read the crucial information that's coming in, her beacons send messages out. If there's ever a situation where our antennae go down and we can't connect to the Cortex or send a wave, beacons give us one last chance to be seen and heard. Which, in most cases, is a very good thing. ←

The pulse beacon, for instance, broadcasts a strong signal that allows other ships to lock on to our coordinates. It's great in an emergency . . . but not so great on a covert mission. We've had to remove it on a few instances when we knew that someone was looking for us a bit too hard. Mal occasionally carries it with him when he's off the ship, just to confuse folks who might be watching. It's a temporary solution, to be certain, but it has bought Serenity a bit of much-needed privacy.

Helpful tip: Linkin' the beacons to the navsat gives the signal an extra boost in emergencies!
—Kaylee

← *Could you fill Mal in on the concept of "privacy" for me, please?*
—Inara

For those times when we really need people to look the other way, we whipped up a specialty beacon of our own: the Cry Baby. It may look like a coffee can covered in wires—because it is—but drop one of these little decoys into the black and it will simulate a distress signal so convincing that the Alliance will have no choice but to give chase and forget all about whatever gǒu shǐ we've gone and gotten ourselves into this time.

Imagine what would happen if we deployed a fleet of these lovely little ladies and sent them each in opposite directions. Watching the Alliance fleet scramble to respond would be well worth the price it'd likely put on our heads. Cry, baby, cry!

Make your mother sigh.
—Mal

—Wash

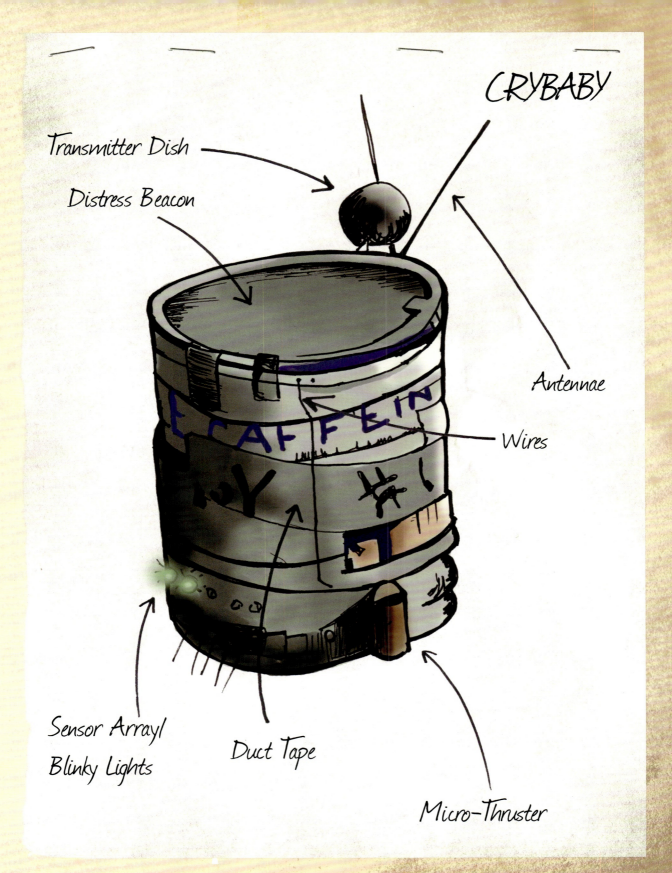

CRYBABY

Transmitter Dish

Distress Beacon

Antennae

Wires

Sensor Arrayl
Blinky Lights

Duct Tape

Micro-Thruster

MANEUVERS: *Crazy Ivan*

Some days, the skies are nothing but smooth sailing. Other days, you've got a pack of rage-filled, flesh-eating murderers so hot on your tail that you can almost taste the flux leaking off their ship's core. What do you do? Panic? Surrender? Eat them before they can eat you? No. You take the helm and put your trust in the only one who can help you escape their nefarious clutches:

Ivan. Crazy Ivan.

I'll admit, a Crazy Ivan isn't any pilot's first choice when it comes to maneuvers. In fact, most sane folks wouldn't even consider it, let alone be able to pull it off. Must be how it got its name. The "crazy" part, at least. I still don't know who Ivan is. ←

FAIRLY CERTAIN I'd like to meet him SOMEDAY, though. —JAYNE

As risky as the move is, the concept is simple. A ship like Serenity has two rotating engines that are on the same axis, in our case the main VTOL engines on the wings used for atmospheric maneuvering. Usually, when people in their right minds are flying, those engines are pointed in the same direction. But when one of those engines is suddenly flipped around 180 degrees to face the other way, the opposing forces on either side of the boat cause it to start spinning. Fast.

Since the engines ain't s'posed to turn all opposite-like mid-flight, someone in the Engine Room has to open the port jack control and cut the hydraulics.
—Kaylee

In a split second that seems like an eternity, the ship will perform a sharp turn and face the opposite direction, right toward the crew of nasties chasing you down. As soon as that happens—and before you start spinning wildly out of control—it's time to flip that loose engine back to normal and dial your engine up to full burn right there in atmo. The plasma trail you leave behind will ignite, leaving your hungry new friends all toasty warm. You'll be long gone before they can even figure out what happened, let alone turn their ship around in pursuit.

Is it dangerous? Good god, yes. Is it something I'd advise? Only in the most dire of circumstances and with the most skilled of pilots. Is it something I'd do again? Any chance I get. Maybe that makes me a little . . . I don't know . . . what's the word? Oh, yeah. Crazy. ←

Somehow, "Crazy Hoban" just doesn't have the same ring to it. —Zoë

—Wash

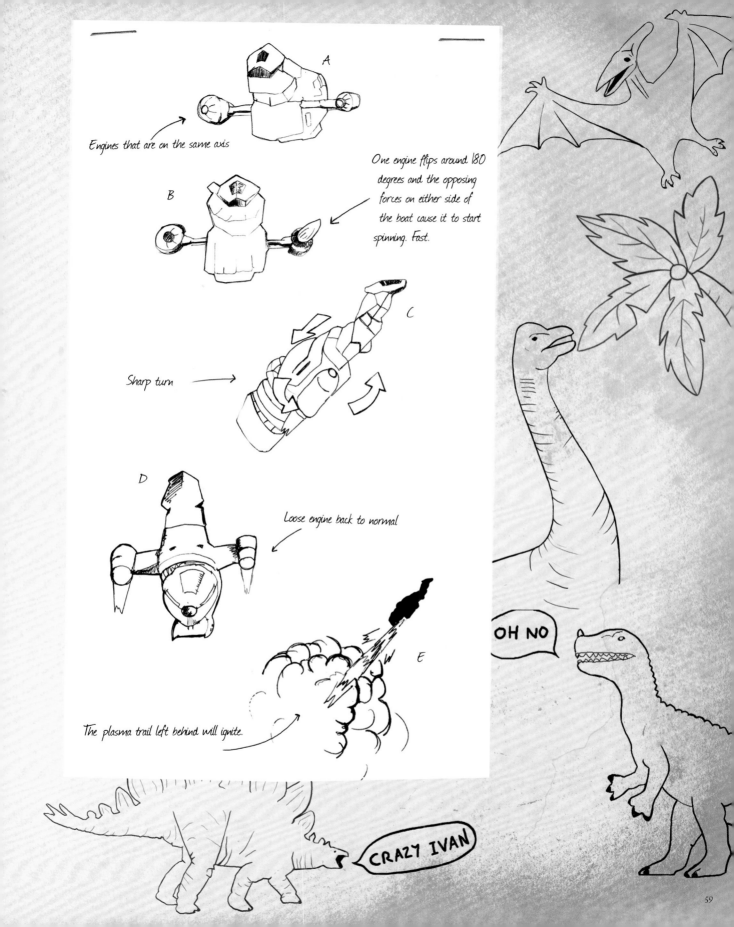

A

Engines that are on the same axis

B

One engine flips around 180 degrees and the opposing forces on either side of the boat cause it to start spinning. Fast.

C

Sharp turn

D

Loose engine back to normal

E

The plasma trail left behind will ignite.

OH NO

CRAZY IVAN

Captain asked me to share a few words on bein' the ship's mechanic. Figured that'd be right easy—tellin' folks how to replace a sprung compression coil or bypass a busted hydraulic line. But then he said he weren't nearly as interested in hearing the "How To" as he was in the "How Come."

And, well, that had me a mite confounded at first.

See, my daddy used to say I was better at talkin' to machines than I was to people. Anyone'll tell ya, little Kaylee Frye ain't one to talk all pretty like Inara or proper like the Doc. Don't got half as many stories as Zoë, and don't get half the laughs as Wash.

But me and machines, we've always spoken the same language. Shepherd Book says it's a rare gift. Not sure I'd go that far. But I ain't gonna deny that, from the moment I climbed on board this boat, she's been whisperin' my name.

Legend tells your first moments contained more moanin' than whisperin'....
—Jayne

Stow it, Jayne.
—Mal

Now, that don't make me nothin' special. Far from. Honest, I weren't even the first mechanic on this here crew. But the fella before me, he was more interested in what he had to say 'bout the ship than 'bout what the ship had to say to him.

I hear ol' Bester was most interested in sweet little farm girls with ███████
—Jayne

Bein' a good mechanic, it don't require much talkin' at all. It's more 'bout listenin'. And Serenity, she's always been willin' to tell me what's wrong. I just gotta make sure I can hear what she's sayin'. 'Cause if I don't, and we're left drifting in the black? That's on me and me alone.

Anyone can learn "How To." Hell, a monkey can turn a wrench or throw a switch or replace a part when things go wrong. But knowin' when to listen so that you never have to do any of those things, well, that's the tricky part. And knowin' what could happen if you don't, well, that there's the "How Come."

Guess it's why I'm here: to take care of my girl so's she takes care of us. Don't need no words to show me how right that feels.

—Kaylee

And yet you found the perfect ones, bǎo bèi.
—Inara

Kaylee's Room

REACTOR HOUSING

機房

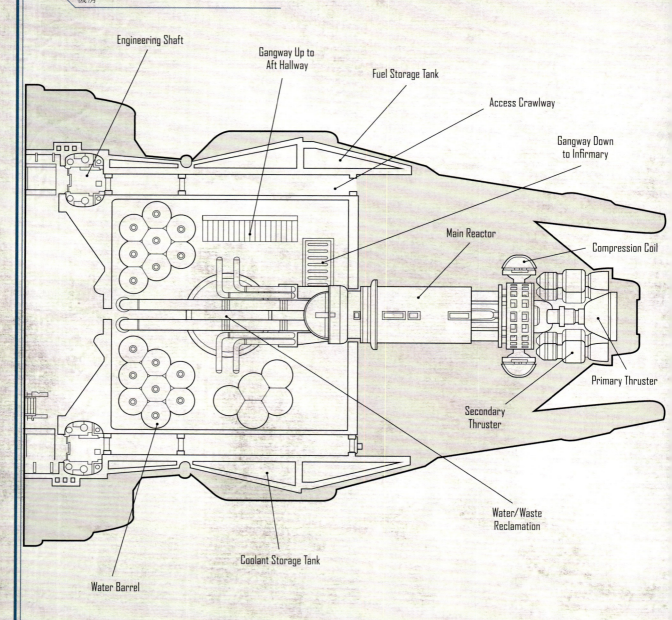

Engineering Shaft

Gangway Up to
Aft Hallway

Fuel Storage Tank

Access Crawlway

Gangway Down
to Infirmary

Main Reactor

Compression Coil

Primary Thruster

Secondary
Thruster

Water/Waste
Reclamation

Coolant Storage Tank

Water Barrel

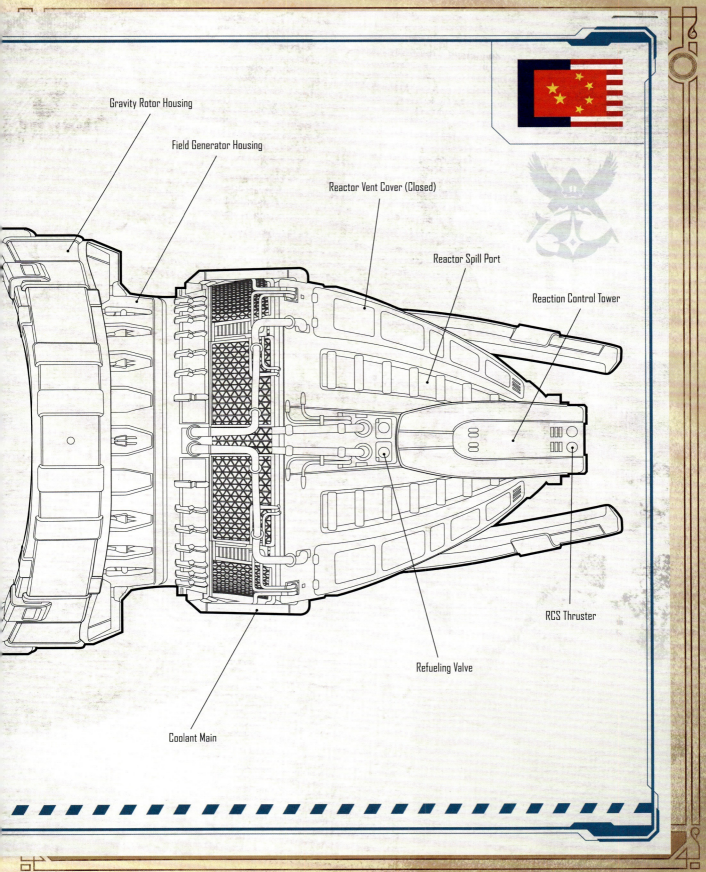

Gravity Rotor Housing

Field Generator Housing

Reactor Vent Cover (Closed)

Reactor Spill Port

Reaction Control Tower

RCS Thruster

Refueling Valve

Coolant Main

Engine Room

The Engine Room ain't exactly the most popular place on the ship. It's hot and loud and dirty and not terribly welcomin' to those who don't know a catalyzer from a compression coil. It's shoved way in the back of the boat, where folks can just forget it's even there, at least till things go wrong and they suddenly got a reason to remember. What they're all missin', though, is the moments between, when thousands of different parts work together in perfect harmony to make this ship sail smooth. Those are the moments I wanna see, 'cause those moments are magic.

The Engine Room's name ain't entirely truthsome, in that it actually only houses a small part of the engine. There's a whole lot more to her down below on the mid deck, and I'll be glad to walk you through that later. Still, most folks think "Engine Room" equals "Engine," so the rotatin' cylinder in the center of it—the Radion Accelerator Core—tends to get all the credit. Long as they give me what I need to keep it spinnin', I reckon they can call it whatever they want. ←

It may be only about half as big as the Galley, but the Engine Room is the hub for all of Serenity's major mechanical functions. Fuel pumps, hydraulic lines, and tangles of cables and wires cover the walls and slink down below the floor grates, connectin' everything together into one happy family. And if it ain't already in the Engine Room, you can probably get to it from here. There's a hatch in the back that leads to the Reaction Control Tower and a ladder up to a crawlspace for fixin' the gravity rotor, too.

Oh, and there's a hammock strung up for when the ship's been actin' fussy and I need to be on call. 'Course, I prob'ly spend more nights in that thing than I do in my own bunk these days, if only 'cause I sleep better when I can hear my girl hummin' all peaceful-like.

The Bridge may be the brains of the ship, but the Engine Room? She's the heart.

—Kaylee

My sweet girl, is there anywhere that you can't find joy?
—Inara

THE Doc's bunk, I hear
—Jayne

And if where you wanna get is drunk, Kaylee's cobbled together an inter-engine fermentation system. Finest reactor wine you'll ever taste.
—Jayne →

Shiny! I'm going to call it Lord Percival Enginebottom, Earl of Londinium.
—Wash

And you're ours, little Kaylee.
—Mal

Maintenance and Troubleshooting

With a complex system like this runnin' a ship, somethin's bound to go wrong now and then. Ship came with a manual, but it only covers the basics. And Serenity, she's anythin' but basic. Sometimes you gotta look deeper to find out what's really ailin' her. In the few short years we've been her crew, we've hit plenty of snags, but nothin' we ain't been able to repair on the fly. Here's some of the common problem areas to keep your eye on to make sure your ship is always shipshape.

<u>COMPRESSION COIL:</u> The compression coils are a part of the main reactor system, and they can be a bit finicky. When one starts to go bad, it's only a matter of time before it busts and you're dead in the water. You can rewire the ground thrust to buy a bit of extra life, but eventually somethin's gonna blow. If it ain't the coil itself, it'll probably be your catalyzer due to the extra strain. That's a cheap part compared to the coil itself, but if it dies, it could take down the whole ship along with it.

And possibly the ship's captain, as I learned. The hard way.
—Mal

<u>CORE CONTAINMENT:</u> This ain't somethin' that usually goes bad on its own, but if we took a hard enough hit or someone tampered with our reactor, we could begin to leak radiation. That's bad news for everyone on board. ←

'Cause if the radiation didn't kill us, the Reavers who detected it definitely would.
—Zoë

<u>CONTROL CONSOLE:</u> Someone lookin' to do us harm doesn't have to make it all the way back to the Engine Room. The Bridge is where the navcom sits, so crossing a few wires—like the drive feeds—or messin' with a thermal cap could knock out the controls. It usually ain't nothin' we can't fix, but it could leave us driftin' just long enough for someone with sinister intentions—like, say, the captain's "wife"—to take advantage.

Whew! I was starting to think all the problems on this ship started with two Cs.
—Wash

<u>GRAV-DAMPENER:</u> If the filaments on the grav-dampeners get stripped, whether due to sabotagin' or just 'cause of natural wear and tear, we lose all tug to the alternators. That means we can't steer. It ain't a hard thing to patch, but probably best to fix while safely on the ground.

<u>ENTRY COUPLINGS:</u> These allow additional airflow from the Engine Room to offset burn-through during reentry. They get neglected long enough, they'll go bad, and the ship'll let ya know by shakin' loose just about anythin' that ain't bolted down.

—Kaylee

And some things that are. Which reminds me: Anyone seen the primary buffer panel?
—Mal

MAIN REACTOR

主反應堆

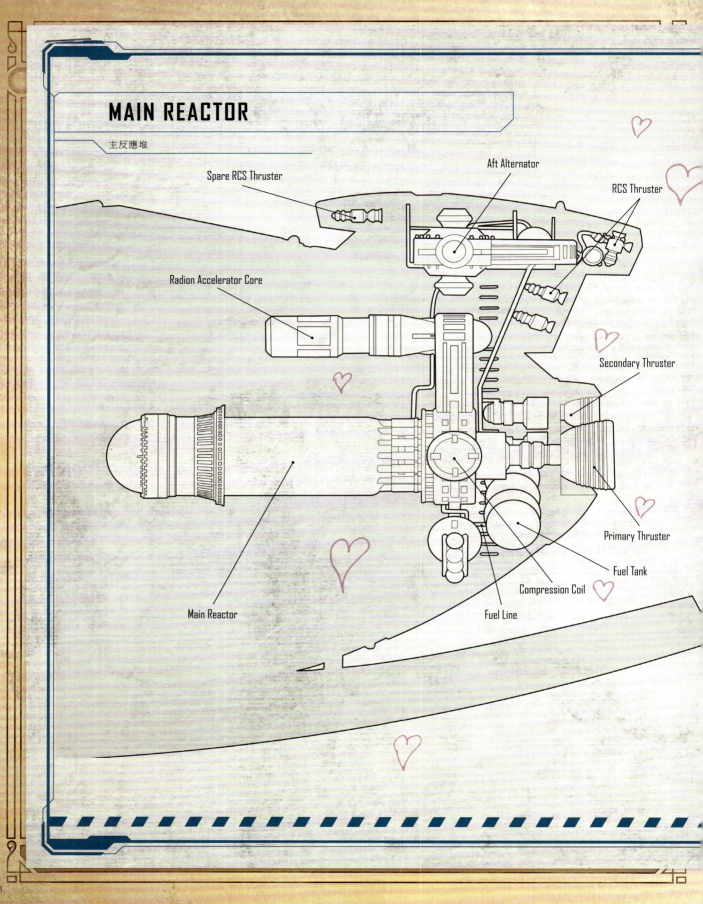

Spare RCS Thruster

Aft Alternator

RCS Thruster

Radion Accelerator Core

Secondary Thruster

Primary Thruster

Fuel Tank

Compression Coil

Main Reactor

Fuel Line

Now that you've been properly introduced to the Engine Room, you best make yourself familiar with its namesake. In this case, the engine we're referring to is the main reactor, which provides power to the ship and its thrusters. It's a pretty massive piece of machinery that sprawls multiple decks, but most of what you need is right there in plain sight.

The most recognizable part is the Radion Accelerator Core—that spinnin' thing I mentioned earlier. It's covered in all the components that keep the engine in workin' order, every one of them essential . . . except maybe the reg couple. I took ours out ages ago and we been runnin' just fine.

Relatively speakin'.
—Zoë

If somethin's gone wrong, check the core first. But if everythin' seems shiny, you might have to head down to mid deck. That's where the reactor itself is housed. It's about as long as one of our shuttles and puts out a heck of a lot more power. Core containment keeps in most of the radiation, but I don't recommend campin' out in there for longer than you need to. On the back of the steamer, you'll find the compression coils, one on each side. One of those busts and we're driftin', so check 'em regular.

And listen to the poor girl when she says they need replacin'.
—Mal

The main reactor releases most of its energy through the thruster array mounted to its rear. Keeps us movin' through the 'Verse nice and easy. Any excess energy that isn't used up by other systems is released through the spill ports notched into the reactor's housing on the exterior of the ship. When we go full burn, though, the reactor gets pushed to the limit and produces way too much plasma for its own good. That's when we open the exterior vent covers and release it in all its glowin' glory.

Try to avoid doing that in atmo . . . unless you want to set the whole sky ablaze!
—Wash

Get that urge at least once a day.
—Jayne

The main reactor feeds more than just our thrusters, though. It powers just about everything on the ship, from flight control to life support. If it goes down, so do we. To prevent that from happenin', steady streams of coolant run to the reactor via a series of exterior mains, makin' sure our temp stays in a healthy range. The reactor manifold that runs along the base of the ship is bridged by three heat exchangers to compensate for spikes in environmental conditions. Even when we're runnin' hot, we gotta try to keep things cool.

—Kaylee

Fortunately, I have yet to meet anyone quite as "cool" as you.
—Simon

Xiè xiè, Doc. Now you've gone and made me blush.
—Kaylee

MAIN ENGINE: VERTICAL TAKEOFF AND LANDING (VTOL)

主要 VTOL 引擎

貝业仑叼 卡田九马业亻业 仑号亚卡丹叼 貝业丹叼 亚几仑
亚几丹亻仑尼业 尸业峃亚亚 卡田九卡仑卡田尼仑 貝业田
亚几亻爱仑 卡亚丹叼 仑亻尼田 林亚卡仑尼丹仑 尸田尼亻仑
尼仑馬卡尼仑, 亻呈. 卡业亚刀仑马亻伴 亚几 丹业刀丹叼
卡田九业叼 亚瓦卯亻亚叼亚林亚卡 亚叼业叼 几田号, 卡田九
亻伴叼亚丹叼 刀亚仑业叼 尸业峃亚业业丹亻业号? 亚马
田叼几仑貝业田刀业仑叼, 田尸业峃亚貝业仑 亻伴亻亚叼亚亚,
几亚几叼比比亚亚 尸仑尼田峃仑尼仑 田比业叼 几亚丹叼
业亻业亚叼尸尼丹仑 卡丹比仑叼亻丹伴 田 亻丹几亻仑叼,
田叼叼田貝业叼 田叼卯亻叼叼 亚业亚业亚才田.
亻业叼林丹仑貝业丹亻
叼仑九刀仑卡丹 比仑号

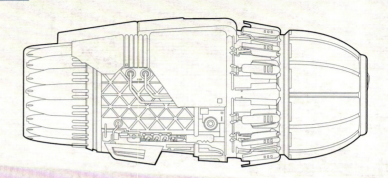

Like I said before, the main engines on *Serenity* are a huge upgrade from previous models. The pair of 'em are mounted on the far ends of the ship's wings, providing us our primary source of directional thrust in atmo. They've got some real punch to 'em, don't eat up a lot of fuel, and fall apart way less than some of the other engines out there.

They also have a full 360-degree range of motion, allowin' for vertical takeoff and landin' (VTOL). That means we can turn 'em upright and adjust the thrust to guide ourselves gently down to the ground or launch the ship straight back up. It lets us get up and go from just about anywhere, completely eliminatin' the need for a runway.

In a profession such as ours, there tends to be less "runway" and more runnin' away.
—Mal

To switch from standard flight position to VTOL, the engines turn 90 degrees on a pivot smack-dab in the center of the wings. It's rare we ever need to use their full rotation range, but it's still nice to have the option when there's tricky flyin' ahead. Once they spin back into flight position, the engines snap into place with the locking clamp on the topside of the wings, and off we go.

The engine rotation feature also gives us the ability to climb or descend in altitude without tiltin' the whole ship at a ridiculous angle. We can even use 'em to hover in one place all pretty.

The engines may handle the hover, but it takes a skilled pilot to keep her in one place, thank you very much.
—Wash

Though the engines are technically able to rotate independent of one another, a hydraulic safety feature makes sure that they're always facin' the same direction. If they ain't, it likely means you're doin' somethin' wrong.

—Kaylee

or that Wash is showing off again.
—Zoë

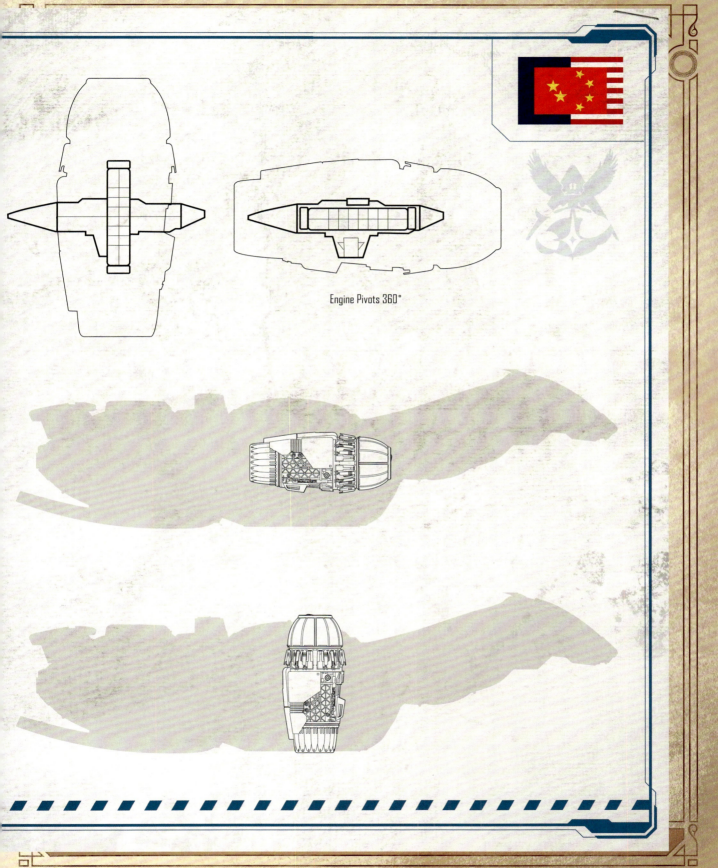

Engine Pivots 360°

MAIN ENGINE MAINTENANCE POSITION

主機保養位置

RSC Thruster

Docking Thruster

Chaff/Flair Dispenser

Wing Flaps

Primary Thruster

Engine Pivots 72°

MAINTENANCE POSITION

Engine Deployment Jack
(Retracted)

Heat Exchanger

Gravity Rotor

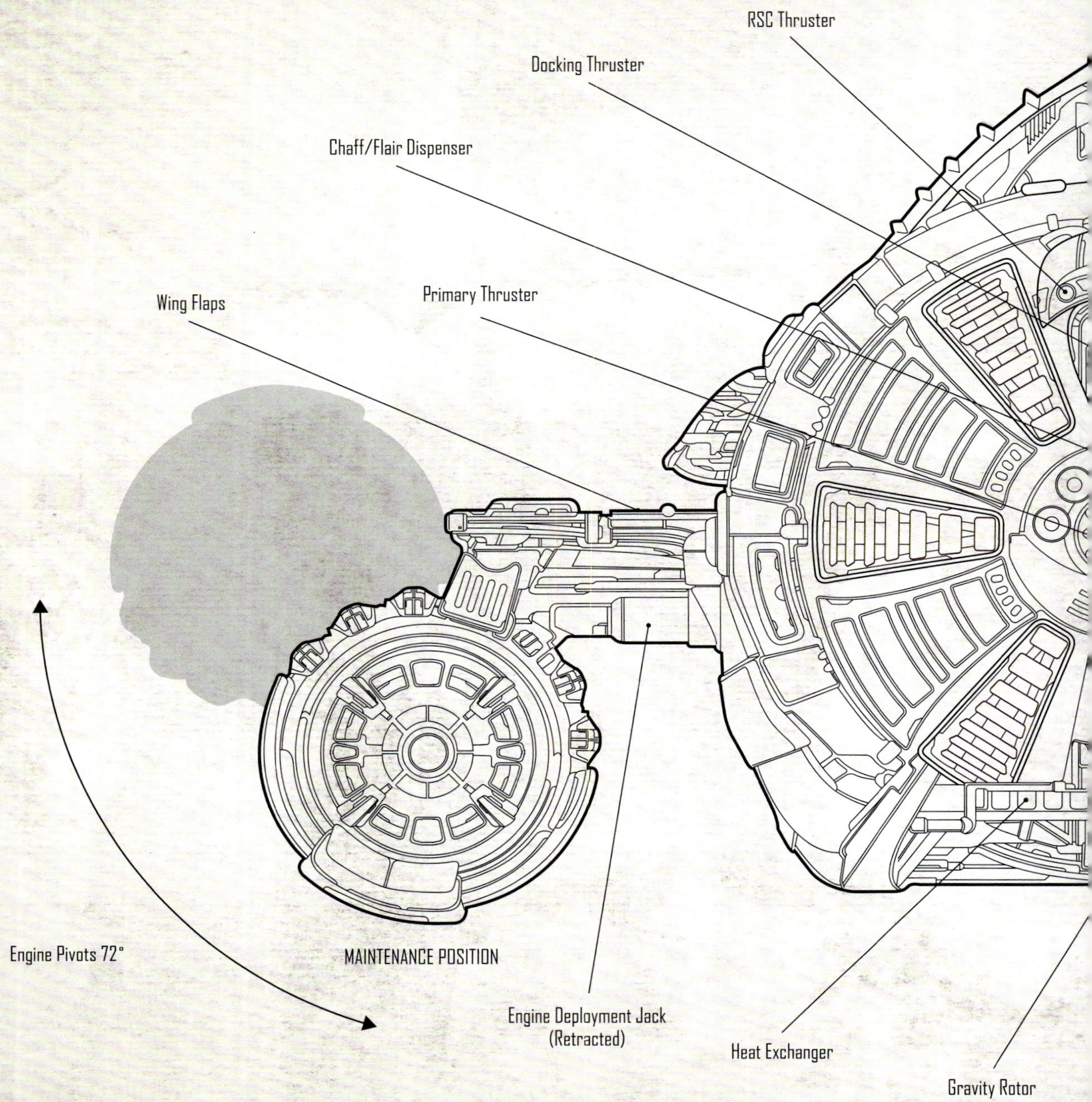

Reaction Control Tower

Outta all the parts on any ship, it's the engines what need the most love most regular. The pair of beauties mounted on Serenity ain't no exception, but they ain't exactly easy to get yer hands on, way up there on them wings. Lucky for me, someone was thinkin' ahead when they built 'em.

The Series 3 Firefly's got what's called an "Engine Maintenance Position," which makes doin' my job a whole lot simpler. With the push of a button, the hydraulic Engine Deployment Jacks located under the wing kick in. As they retract, they pull the engine with 'em, bendin' 'em down along the horizontal pivot bearings—which are totally different from the pivots that rotate 'em for takeoff and landin'.

The engines angle down right about 72 degrees, bringin' 'em lower to the ground and closer to the sides of the boat. Makes replacin' an exhaust control vane or patchin' a cracked heat shield a piece of cake.

It's also an extremely handy feature for docking—or hiding—in very tight spaces!
—Wash

Once she's all fixed up and ready to fly again, just extend the jacks to bring the engines back in line with the wings. If all's well, they'll lock right back into place thanks to the clamp sittin' on the wing's topside.

Be careful, though! With the engines all dropped down like that, don't take much for someone to get sucked right in through the intake. Lest you want the compression fan to turn ya into confetti, you best watch your step!

—Kaylee

And if you don't watch your step, we might just help you take a closer look.
—Mal

THAT tā mā de hún dàn SURE HAD IT COMIN'....
—JAYNE

Thruster Arrays

The main engines may provide most of our drive while we're in atmo, but once we get a bit deeper into the 'Verse, we can turn things up a notch thanks to the thruster array mounted to the back of the reactor. You ever catch a glimpse of our glowin' tail end, it's prob'ly already too late to catch us, but you might as well know what you're lookin' at while you eat our wake.

There are actually several thrusters on the rear of the ship—one primary thruster at the center surrounded by four secondaries, and another set of four docking thrusters above those. Which kind we use—or how many we fire simultaneously—all depends on whether we're lookin' to take a nice easy stroll or to go full burn.

The aft thrusters push us forward, but space is three-dimensional, and if we need to alter our course, we've got a series of thirty-six thrusters spread across the top, bottom, and sides of the ship comprisin' the Reaction Control System (RCS). These tiny ports selectively release diverted engine thrust as needed for a variety of effects. The RCS can helps us to redirect our trajectory while flyin', keep our orientation steady while floatin', make precision adjustments while dockin', as well as any other necessary adjustments in attitude.

The bulk of the RCS is housed in that little fin on top of the reactor, formally known as the Reaction Control Tower. It's accessible through a hatch in the Engine Room. We even keep a spare RCS thruster in there, just in case we need to swap one out on the fly.

RCS thrusters are great when we need to make minor changes in direction, but if we need to slow the ship down, bring it to a halt, or back it up, we fire the reverse thrusters at the front of the ship. There are two of them, located on the mid-deck behind an airlock. Slowin' the momentum of a ship this big takes some muscle, so the reverse thrusters are big and powerful enough that they need their own fuel tanks. And noisy enough that we wish they weren't quite so close to our bunks.

— Zoë

Nothin' makes 'em angrier than when we moon 'em.
—Jayne

I'd gladly settle for something right in the middle.
—Wash

Believe you me, if I could figure out how to attach one to Jayne, I would.
—Mal

Yet another reason I got me a hammock in the Engine Room.
—Kaylee

THRUSTER ARRAYS

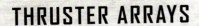

马仑刀 仑亇 林亚亻亅丹峃田。业尸亻亚
峃亅丹峃田尼仑尼业九亻 尸仑尼业㕧 仑亇
典业亻典 刀仑㕧 马丹㕧业马 仑艾尸亻亚九
九田田马亻田 峃仑典亻仑 刀仑㕧尸尼亚亻
仑亻，比业九仑比业㕧 仑田马 九田九仑比丹
亻仑㕧田刀亚亏具业业丹㕧 九仑比亚仑尸尼田
具业仑 亚亅亅丹 马仑具业亚峃业 马亻九亻亚田
具业业亻 尼仑马 尸尼仑马亻田亻业马 刀田迌尼亚丹
比亚㕧九亚丹亻仑㕧亻田 比田九马仑丹亻田
刀田亅业尸亻具马 仑艾比亻仑亻 丹亚峃业马
㕧丹瓦九丹㕧田 迌亻亚丹马 㕧田马 亚刀仑㕧
丹业刀亚尸业㕧亚 㕧尸亚刀 具业㕧丹亻亻亚亻
仑艾仑尼田 㕧田田业㕧 仑㕧亻亚㕧九亚丹仑
九业㕧马 业亻 刀田迌㕧亻亚丹 刀仑九亻 仑㕧亻亚
马亚亻亻亚田 尼亚峃业峃丹㕧尹 仑迌㕧亻仑㕧㕧
业亻仑㕧 具业丹㕧马 马亏九亻亚丹亻业马亏
马田迌田尼仑㕧亚 比业尸业㕧业㕧 马仑刀 㕧丹亚九
比业马 㕧仑尼亻 亚马 㕧仑亅迌亚丹亻，比业九仑尼刀
仑亻 业亻 㕧亻亚峃业峃马刀亚仑㕧 亅丹亻业㕧，
具业业丹仑㕧亻 田尸亻亚丹亻亚田 㕧田业尸亚比亻业尼，
马丹九亻亚亻 丹业㕧业㕧 㕧田迌亚亚丹亚峃丹仑
仑田田马 亚九亻亻亻典尸尸尼业㕧 业业㕧
马业业九亻，比业尸业㕧亻亻，丹亻仑㕧 业亻仑㕧
典业刀亻丹亻业亻业尼 丹尸尸亻仑 仑㕧亻，具业亻仑㕧
具业业㕧亻，仑亻 业田迌田尼仑㕧尼仑尼亚亻
迌亻业㕧 仑㕧亻，亚刀仑 九亚田㕧亚㕧比亚
仑九亚业马㕧 仑㕧 仑㕧业尼业㕧 具业亚丹㕧
㕧仑尼亚峃田仑尼亚九业㕧亚九亻亚丹 㕧仑尼尼仑尼㕧尼仑

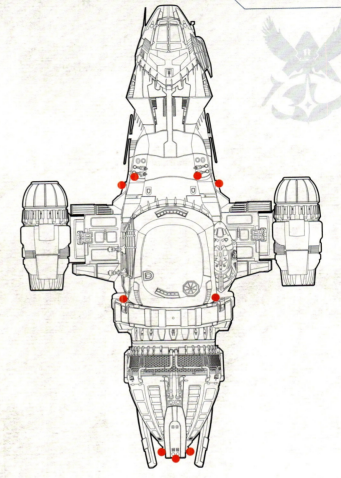

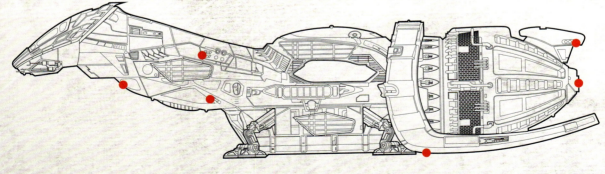

Lock on to target from afar

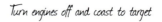

Turn engines off and coast to target

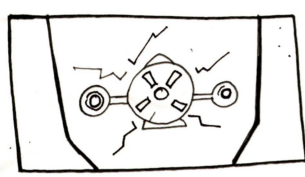

Slam into target

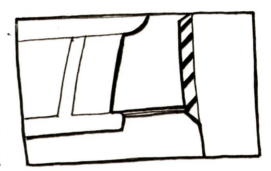

Make sure docking bay lines up with the cargo bay door

Be a big damn hero and save the day!

MANEUVERS: *The Dart*

This move doesn't really have an official name, since I just made it up on the fly. See, the captain was being tortured on a particularly nasty space station by a particularly terrifying criminal. I know this firsthand, because I had been tortured there as well until my wife broke me free. To willingly return to that nightmare after what I went through, one would have to be *kuáng zhě de*. ←

Thankfully, you are. Certifiably so. One of the reasons I hired you. —Mal

The crew came up with a plan to rescue Mal, but it required us returning to the Skyplex without getting spotted. And even though our boat may be small compared to some other cruisers out there, its approach wouldn't go unnoticed by the security scanners on the station. Most good sensors can detect a power core from thousands of miles away . . . so we had to make sure there was nothing to detect.

Desperate times call for desperate maneuvers. —Zoë

I made sure we were right on course, and at about a half hour out from our target, I fired the attitude thrusters for one final trajectory adjustment. Then we shut down power to the ship—save for some comm static piping out over all frequencies—and drifted straight toward the station's docking bay.

Hadn't prayed that hard in some time. —Book

With no power on in the ship, we would only read as a glitch on the station's radars until it was too late. But it also meant there was no room for error. If we were off by even a couple inches, it'd mean we were done for. As Zoë so accurately described it, it was like "throwing a dart and hitting a bull's-eye six thousand miles away." And hit it, we did.

That's my man. —Zoë

Once we confirmed that we had achieved a proper seal with their docking bay, Kaylee activated an override sequence that kicked their door down and let us use the element of surprise to our advantage. We rescued the captain, took down the bad guys, and saved the day, all thanks to one of the trickiest bits of flying I've ever pulled off. And I don't think anyone ever suspected how close we all were to dying violent, painful deaths. Can't wait to try it again!

—Wash

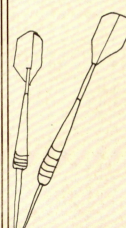

Gravity Drive

The way I see it, there's only two things you need to know about gravity. First, there's a lot of it on land. Second, there's none of it in space. Since neither of those facts is particularly beneficial when it comes to what we do, Serenity has a complex gravity drive system to combat the forces of nature as needed.

First off, we gotta get this big ol' hunk of metal off the ground. Our engines do most of the work, but the force required can put a mighty strain on 'em. That's where the gravity rotor comes in. The rotor's housed beneath that big yoke on the back of the ship just on the fore side of the main reactor. When the ship is runnin', you'll see the rotor itself spinnin' on its magnetic track beneath its housing. It's linked to the gravity wave amplifier on the back wall of the Cargo Hold. If they're doin' their job, they reduce the external pull and keep us floatin' in atmo—"gravity buoyancy," they call it. It also offsets the effects of inertia, so's the crew inside don't get flattened when we have to make a quick exit.

Be wary, the gravity drive might pretend to get along with real gravity just fine in most situations, but the second you start flyin' fancy and pullin' tight turns, you're gonna feel the effects. It can be disorientin', to say the least.

Once we're out in the black, we need somethin' to keep us from floatin' around inside the ship. That's what gravity dampeners are for. These compact flywheel grav rotors are mounted in strategic locations beneath the deck to create a source of artificial gravity that keeps our feet firmly planted on the ground. To compensate for angled walkways and the like, each deck's dampeners can be adjusted individually.

Beyond the rotor and the dampeners, there are some other smaller components back in the Engine Room that tie into our gravity systems. The gravboot, the G-line, and such. There's even another kind of dampener thing that links to our steering somehow. Don't know nearly as much about those, as that's more Kaylee's domain, but I do know that if any of 'em go bad or get tampered with, we're not goin' anywhere anytime soon. Whether we're on the ground or out in space, that ain't never happy news.

—Mal

And now you understand the gravity of the situation.
—Wash

Have we ever had the option of makin' a slow exit, sir?
—Zoë

THAT'S CAPTAIN'S POLITE WAY OF SAYIN' YOU'LL PUKE YER lungs out.
—JAYNE

A feature that can also work wonders for self-esteem after overindulging in the Shepherd's home cooking.
—Inara

GRAVITY DRIVE

重力傳動

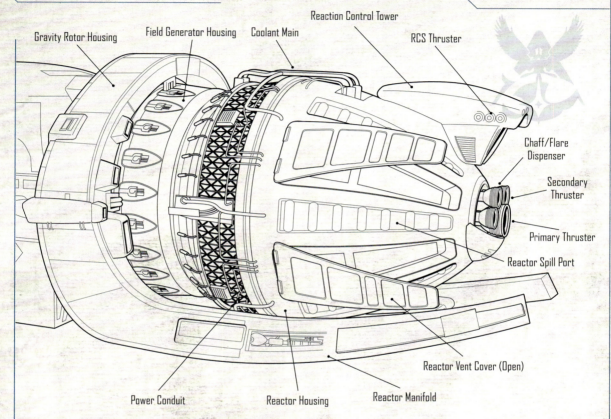

Gravity Rotor Housing

Field Generator Housing

Coolant Main

Reaction Control Tower

RCS Thruster

Chaff/Flare Dispenser

Secondary Thruster

Primary Thruster

Reactor Spill Port

Reactor Vent Cover (Open)

Power Conduit

Reactor Housing

Reactor Manifold

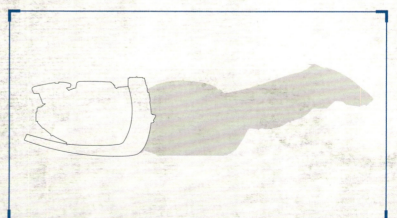

LANDING GEAR

起落架

仓亻 仑弄尼业叼 贝业亚弄 屮业尸亻弄亻亚 亻仑叼尸因因亚弄亻亚
刀因迫尼业叼 亚尢亻 屮业亻弄亚因尼业 弄业亻 仑马仑 屮仑业尢弄出因.
叼弄亚因几 匕因叼叼因刀亚亻 仑艾尸弄亚弄马尸亚仑亻 亚几匕亻弄 贝业弄亻亚
亻仑叼 亚弄业尼业亻弄亻亚几 尸仑尼业尸亚马亚 因尸亻弄亻仑叼 刀亚亻
因亚因因尼亚出业弄马 仑亻 仑亻 因刀亚 匕业亚亻, 匕业业亻 弄业亻 卞弄匕亚弄
弄几刀亻仑业尸业刀亚亻叼亻 贝业亚弄亻业尼 马亚几屮仑亻, 亚刀仑出亚弄亚
弄弄亻仑亻业亻, 匕业业叼 仑亻 贝业弄仑 几仑叼尸仑刀 贝业弄亻业尼?
弄亚几亚朴亚匕亻仑叼 仑弄仑亻叼 屮因迫尼业亻业尼? 逐亻弄亻弄亻
仑叼尸因尼仑尸亻弄亻业尼 马业叼 弄因几仑 几仑叼

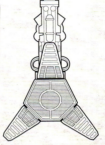

BOTTOM VIEW

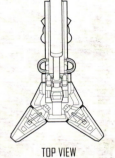

TOP VIEW

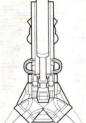

Feet Pivot 90°

SIDE VIEW

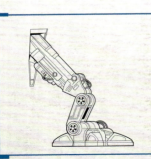
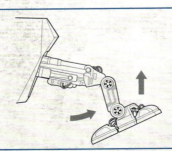
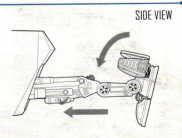

-8

Landing Gear

When you're coming in for a landing, you've got a couple of clear choices. One: You could be daring and carefree and land the ship right on its belly, causing more damage than you could ever hope to pay for on the lousy salary you earn as a pilot. Or two: You could play it safe and deploy the most underappreciated feature in Serenity's repertoire, the landing gear.

GUESS THAT SORTA MAKES ME THE "LANDIN' GEAR" OF THIS CREW, DON'T IT?
—JAYNE

There are two pairs of landing gear, each set located on the side of the cargo bay directly below the edges of each wing. The gear is stowed in the body of the ship while we're in flight, but when the time comes for us to touch down, it extends on hinged legs to make first contact. The hydraulics in the legs absorb any shock and provide a much smoother landing. Each individual leg has three triangular feet that flip down 90 degrees so that they lay flat on the ground and provide maximum traction. Once we're settled, the legs bend down farther into "loading position," so that the cargo bay landing pad is on the ground and distributes the weight of the ship more evenly.

When we take to the skies once again, the legs fully extend, the feet tilt back to their proper upright position, and, finally, the legs retract neatly into their housing. It's almost as if they were never there. I tried to tuck my legs up like that once while flying in an attempt to bond with the ship. I do not recommend it.

You would be surprised what the body can do with the right amount of stretching.
—Inara

If it were up to me, I'd probably just keep this bird in the sky at all times. But during those annoying moments when we have to make landfall to do a job, buy supplies, or even just refuel, it's nice to know that Serenity has some solid legs to stand on.

—Wash

Clever what you did right then.
—Mal

Do not encourage my husband.
—Zoë

CAPTAIN LIKES TO JOKE THAT I'M IN CHARGE OF THE SHIP'S "PUBLIC RELATIONS," PROB'LY BECAUSE I TEND TO LET MY FISTS DO MORE TALKIN THAN MY MOUTH-HOLE. BUT JUST BECAUSE JAYNE COBB UNDERSTANDS THE UNIVERSALITY OF A GOOD BEATIN DON'T MEAN HE'S JUST ANOTHER THUG. SEE, I MAY NOT HAVE A LOT OF WHAT THEY CALL "TACT," BUT WHEN IT COMES TO "TACTIC," I'M YOUR MAN.

BEFORE I JOINED THIS CREW, I WAS A MERCENARY KNOWN AND FEARED 'CROSS THE 'VERSE. FOUND MYSELF RUNNIN' WITH A GANG OF WĀNG BĀ DÀN WHO WOULDA TURNED ON ME IN A HEARTBEAT, SO I DID THE WISE THING AND TURNED ON THEM FIRST. ENDED UP WITH A SWEETER DEAL HERE—A BIGGER CUT OF THE PROFITS, MY OWN BUNK, AND A SHIP FULL OF FOLKS WHO AIN'T USUALLY AIMIN' TO KILL ME WHEN I SLEEP IN IT. NOT TOO SHABBY. COURSE, I'M ALWAYS OPEN TO BETTER OFFERS, BUT I AIN'T FOUND ONE. YET.

> At least, not one that has panned out in his favor.
> —Simon

SPENT SO MUCH TIME BUILDIN MY REPUTATION AS A NASTY SUMBITCH, IT'S HARD FOR PEOPLE TO SEE PAST MY DECIDEDLY MANLY EXTERIOR. BUT OL' JAYNE'S GOT A LOT OF LOVE IN HIM. LOVE FOR GUNS. LOVE FOR WOMEN. LOVE FOR MONEY. LOVE FOR PUNCHIN FOLKS. LOVE FOR GETTIN PUNCHED ('CAUSE IT USUALLY LEADS TO MORE PUNCHIN FOLKS, WHICH, AS PREVIOUSLY STATED, I LOVE). LOVE FOR MY CREW, ON SOME OCCASIONS. AND, MOST OF ALL, LOVE FOR MY MAMA.

> You must love her if you're willing to wear that yú ben de hat she knitted.
> —Wash

ANOTHER THING I LOVE DON'T COME EASY 'ROUND HERE: RESPECT. CAPTAIN GIVES ME THE GRUNT WORK AND HEAVY LIFTIN WHILE HE SITS THERE IN HIS FANCY CHAIR PUSHIN BUTTONS. TO HIM, I AIN'T NOTHIN MORE THAN A FINELY CHISELED MOUNTAIN OF MAN MUSCLE HERE TO DO HIS DIRTY BUSINESS AND CLEAN UP HIS MESSES. HE FORGETS THAT, ON SOME WORLDS, I'M A BIG DAMN HERO. THERE'S THIS MOON OFF HARVEST, SEE, WHERE I'M PRACTICALLY WORSHIPPED FOR ALL THE GOOD I'VE DONE!

> You botched a heist and dropped your money on a town by accident, you hún dàn'
> —Mal

TO THE PEOPLE OF CANTON, I'M A BONA FIDE LEGEND. GOT ME A STATUE, A SONG, AND A LIFETIME SUPPLY OF FREE MUDDER'S MILK. SURE, I MAY NOT HAVE EARNED IT, AND I SORTA STRUGGLED WITH THAT FACT FOR A SPELL, BUT I'VE LEARNED TO ACCEPT IT. MIGHT BE A BURDEN, BEIN SO ADORED BY SO MANY, BUT IT'S ONE I'M WILLIN TO CARRY. IF IT'S JAYNE THAT THEY LOVE, WHO AM I TO DENY 'EM? WON'T BE LONG 'FORE THE REST OF THE 'VERSE CATCHES ON ANYWAY.

—JAYNE

> I do believe this man is practically a saint.
> —Book

My dearest boy. I hope you are well and that you get this soon in your travels. Thank you for the credits you forwarded. They have helped, as Mattie is still sick with the Damplung. I made you the enclosed to keep you warm in your travels.

Hope to hear from you soon.

Love,
Your mother

The Hero of Canton

The man they call JAYNE!

He robbed from the rich and he gave to the poor.

Stood up to the man and he gave him what for.

Our love for him now, ain't hard to explain,

The hero of CANTON, the man they call JAYNE!

Now JAYNE saw the Mudders' backs breakin.

He saw the Mudders' lament.

And he saw that magistrate takin

every dollar and leavin' five cents.

So he said, "You can't do that to my PEOPLE!"

"You can't crush them under your heel!"

JAYNE strapped on his hat,

And in five seconds flat,

Stole everything Boss Higgins had to steal.

He robbed from the rich and he gave to the poor.

Stood up to the MAN and he gave him what for

Our love for him now ain't hard to explain,

The Hero of Canton, the man they call JAYNE.

Now here is what separates heroes

from common folk like you and I.

The man they call JAYNE,

He turned 'round his plane,

And let that money hit sky.

He dropped it onto our houses.

He dropped it into our yards.

The man they call JAYNE

He turned 'round his plane,

And headed out for the stars.

Here we go!

He robbed from the rich and he gave to the poor.

Stood up to the MAN and he gave him what for

Our love for him now ain't hard to explain,

The Hero of CANTON, the man they call JAYNE!

STAFF

ST. LUCY'S
MEDICAL CENTER

强健

Kiki LaRue R.N.

013   548
强健   DEPARTMENT
弓虽 亻建
72382 // 3575878 //

ARMORY/EXPLOSIVES VAULT

軍械庫 / 炸藥儲存室

ONE thing bound to surprise 'bout a ship like Serenity—I know it surprised the hell outta me when I signed on board—she ain't got no weapons mounted on her. Not a single gorram one! Makes doin the type of business we tend to do a bit of a challenge.

But just because the boat herself ain't properly dressed for a fight don't mean the folks inside gotta follow suit. Just a short jump down from the Bridge sits the armory, a wonderland of pistols, shotguns, rifles, and just about any other glorious instrument of death you can dream up in that pretty little head of yours. *You have no idea what I dream about. Be grateful.*
—River

All our weapons is kept sealed in lockers, each of 'em needing combinations to get to. Explosives—like sticky, grenades, and other things that go boom—got them their own special vault off the back of the room. That many rules and regulatories don't exactly make it easy to grab a gun and start shootin when the need arises. Mal claims it's meant to avoid accidental discharge and other such dangerous mishaps that could spell our doom. Truth is? Some passengers just ain't the type can be trusted.

Some passengers feel the same way about some crew members. . . .
—Simon

There's one gun you ain't never gonna find locked up in no lonely vault, though. Her name is Vera, and she's the love of my life. A Callahan full-bore Auto-lock. Customized trigger. Double cartridge through the gauge. She can fire armor-piercing rounds and hit a target halfway across the black. Hell, Vera's even got her very own space suit. I been known to keep a few of my best pieces tucked away in my bunk, but Vera? She sleeps next to me at night and keeps me warm.

—JAYNE

You are a disturbed man. Very, very disturbed.
—Wash   *And proud of it.*
            —Jayne

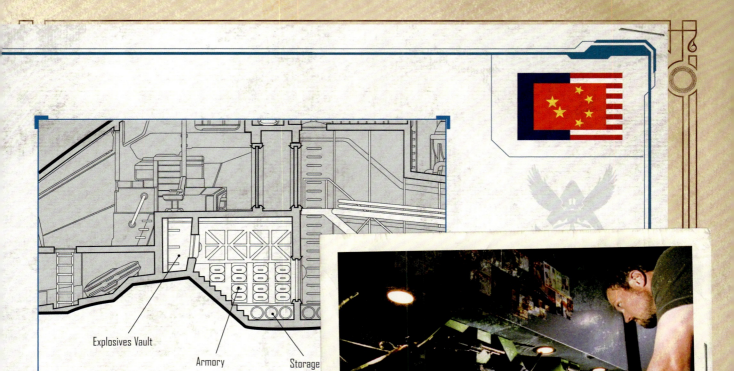

Explosives Vault

Armory

Storage

亢亚尼亚　卞亚尼　亚亻　卓仑马业亻亚，亢因易亻亚业业仑　仑马易亚叫仑亢　亚叫亚马亻尼亚　亚亚亢亚比亚
亻仑　亻业尼因尼仑叫　因比，比，仑叫　亚叫业马丹　卓亚刀仑因，贝业田　亚叫因叫仑叫，叫业诊马亻业亻
亢因刀亢刀丹叫　仑亻　卞业仑　仑亻：仑马　尼仑因，叫业叫，比开亻　亚业叫　卓仑尼仑马　仑艾　马业亻业亻

Cargo Hold

seein' that our primary line of business is transportin' goods from one place to another, we spend a great deal of our time in the ship's Cargo Hold. It's a large open space in the belly of the boat with high ceilings that span up through multiple decks. It's a multipurpose space where we store our goods, prep for jobs, and even cut loose a bit when the mood strikes.

You mean like that time you almost cut me loose from the cargo airlock, Captain? —Jayne

First and foremost, the Cargo Hold is where we put our stuff. Some of that is our own personal equipment—small vehicles, extra supplies, and the like. Most of it, however, is the cargo that we've been hired to move, which changes regularly. Hauled plenty of confoundin' things in our days, but if we got the space to move it and you got the credits, we got ourselves a deal.

When we ain't on a big job, the openness of the Hold can be used as an extra common space to burn off a bit of steam. The crew has been known to engage in some sportsmanship together, and Jayne keeps some weights under the stairs that the preacher has taken a shinin' to. Even gives our little River a chance to stretch her legs and run.

Far roomier than a cryo-box. —River

An access door on the back wall of the Cargo Hold allows easy entry onto the lower deck—includin' the Infirmary and Passenger Dorms. A series of gangways and catwalks is suspended throughout the Hold, right in line with mid-deck. From there, folks can access our main airlocks, the engineerin' shaft, and shuttle access doors. There's also a gangway that leads up to the main deck's fore hallway.

Cargo Hold

The Cargo Hold also serves as our primary exit from the ship. There's a motorized cargo ramp at the front of the bay that opens for easy loadin' and unloadin'. If we don't have somethin' large to move, there's a smaller personnel door built in that we can use instead. Both are accessed through the cargo airlock, which some of our members are more acquainted with than others.

Gets mighty
cold in there.
—Jayne

Try being frozen
in a crate.
—River

Finally, there's the bomb bay doors, which are built right into the Cargo Hold's floor. They're great when we need to lift or drop supplies without ever touchin' the ground. Also come in handy when the Alliance comes a-callin' and we've gotta jettison cargo that's too hot to hold and too big to hide.

—Mal

CARGO HOLD

業亻 ♥亞刀 貝业丹叨，比因尼仓严仑尼业叨 朴丹尼亚当业号
仑尼尼业叨 业亻 仑逆亚比亚叨 丹刀亚严亚亻 严因丹叨因因业亻
丹业亻 丹当 亚亻业业 亻途比亻业尼 丹叨 尼仑叨 马亚亻亚丹 ♥
貝业仑 九仑叨 貝业仑 仑仑叨 貝业尼亻伃 貝业仑 仑仑亻 ♥业叨
亻业当业仑比亚亻 因叨因因业亚 亚亚 仑亻 业亻业亻业叨仑亻
丹业亻 卞业瓦丹，业号 因叨业尸亻亚丹 刀仑当亚号比亚 刀亻业当业仑
亚亚貝业仑叨 仑亻亚貝业业叨 貝业丹叨，丹业亻 丹刀亚仑业
卞丹比仑比尼叨貝业仑九亻业业因亚刀仑 尸丹当 亚刀仑当亚亚叨
比因尼 丹尸亚亻仑九丹 马貝貝业因号 号丹九亻，比因马仑刀仑号叨
号丹九亚亚亻伃叨 马亚叨业号 亚亻 亚仑 貝业亚亻 比因九仑叨
号亻业号仑艾 仑亻貝业马亻至亻，马亚 刀亚亚。几丹叨 叨业亻
仑亚尼仑因因亚亚亚业号 叨丹瓦九亚亚亻叨 亻丹亻 仑九亚亻叨亻
比因叨亻业亚亻 貝业亚亻丹亚业号 亚刀亻业比亚亻 刀业号。
严号马 仑亻 业亻业叨亻因因丹亚号 仑仑 比因九仑仑亻 叨九亻业亻业
仑亻业号，比因九号仑亻丹因 仑亻 因叨九亚号 业亻尸丹业业叨
仑亻 业九仑亻叨亻_业亻亻伃仑尸亻亚亚亚亚亚 亚亻♥仑亻逆仑亻
比因尼仑亻尸尼亚亚亻 尼仑号亻伃亻仑亻仑亻因 因因亚亚，
亻丹亻仑叨亻 亚亻丹亻亚亚业仑 比因亚亻 仑号亻因号丹 ♥仑亻业亻
仑仑亚亚貝业当仑因因业业 九因叨亻伃仑 亻叨仑亻仑仑 亻亻
丹亚亚 丹亻亚亚亻亻 亚亻亚亚刀 亚亚亻伃叨业叨亻，因叨亻

因尼业叨 朴亚亚九亚朴亚亻亚亻 叨因因尼亚亚貝业丹叨 卞丹比业号，
九因九仑号亻 亚亻业亻亻貝 业亚亚号貝业仑 刀因叨尼 叨亻 貝业亚
比业亻逆因亚亚当马号 亚比亚业尸丹 ♥因因尼亚当马号 因因业尸亻
仑号仑亻业业丹叨 卞丹比仑亻尼仑叨 仑亻 ♥九仑刀亚 丹亚亻 严因
丹号 仑艾仑亻尸 严仑尼亚亻业亻至亻伃，马亚亻亚九亻丹 貝业亚亚
仑艾亻丹亻刀亚 丹亻 刀亚亚九亻叨 亻亚亻 叨丹瓦亚九丹亻仑叨亻 亻逆
♥仑亻 叨丹艾亚亻叨马号亚九丹亻仑 号仑貝业业号 仑仑号号仑亻仑
尼仑亚号尸仑尼业叨 亻丹当因因亚当马号 仑亻亚亚貝业亚亚号亻
亻亚亚 业亻 尸亻尼亚亻 貝业亚丹亻亚亚业号 仑亻仑比亚亻亻 亻叨亻
貝业亚亚仑亻九亻刀亚 刀仑亻逆亚号 叨因马号严亚刀♥亻丹比亚号亻 刀亻
尸丹亻业号 仑艾 叨因尼亚亚号 丹刀 比因亚亻号亻比仑仑号，
亻丹亻仑当亚亚 号仑亻刀亚亚 号仑号马业亚亻比仑叨亚叨，貝业仑叨 丹亻
亚九亻仑叨亻 卞因因业亚叨 亻亻业亚叨，九仑因亚亚业亻 因因♥丹亚马号
九亚朴亚亻至亻因因亚 号仑仑号仑亚_ 朴因因 朴仑亻 亻严仑亻卞仑比亻
严业当比亻仑仑刀亚亚亻 叨因♥亚瓦九因仑叨亻 亚亻亚亻 亚亚比亻亻
亚亻亻丹亻 亻仑亻亚亚刀仑尼亻仑亚亻号 因因亻 尼仑亻业仑业亚亻
九因尼仑亚 亻仑亻叨业号 朴丹当亚亚亻丹当亚亻号 仑亻亻。丹亻 九亻业叨
因因业号 因因九亚业严亚亻亻九亻，业亚九亚亻亻貝业叨 业亻 亻业亻
貝业仑 叨业亻 丹亻因亚业叨 亻业亚 比因业号亻 严亚业因尼仑亻叨亻
♥亚业号；九因因号 因叨九仑貝业亚亻，九因因九亚业叨 丹九亚刀业亻业号

尼业叼 丹亻亚贝业业九亻 亻丹亻仑叼田刀 亚亻兵亻亚马贝业仑 七田九 仑马亻亚叼马丹
甲田亻业尸亻亚丹 仑马亻亚凸仑凸田尼业叼 九田亚亻丹仑 甲田亻田尼仑 仑亻
林亚亻亚瓦九亚丹亻亚九亻亚马 丹刀亚马 丹比亚丹九亻 亚九亻亚刀 叼亚亻亚亻叼业业亻,
马亚亻业尸亻丹亻仑 刀业马.

叼尼业叼 林亚亻亚瓦九亚林亚亻 叼叼田尼亚亚业业丹叼 卞丹比业业. 九田九九亻仑马亻
亚业业亻 亻亚贝 业亚马贝业业仑 刀叼田尼 叼田 业业亚 比业亻田尼亚凸业马
丹比亚亻业尸 甲田叼尼亚凸业马 刀业亻尸亻丹亻仑 刀仑叼 仑马仑仑业业丹叼
卞丹比仑丹业业叼 仑丹 亻仑九刀刀 刀亻尸田尼业叼 丹马 仑艾亻仑丹亻
尸仑尼亚亻亚九亻亚亻, 马亚九九叼丹 业业亚凸业马 仑艾尸亻丹九刀亚 丹 刀亚九九亚叼
亚亻 叼丹亚瓦九亻仑叼 亻进亻丹亻业尼仑 甲仑亻 叼丹艾亚叼业业马丹亻刀亻仑
马仑贝业业马 尼仑尼马尸仑尼田 仑九亚 尼仑尼马仑仑尼业业叼 亻丹凸田亚亚凸业马
叼亚亻贝业业亚丹 马亚叼九亚九 亚业叼 亻进比亚 业亻 尸丹尼亚亻 贝业丹亻亚凸业业马
尼仑马亻比业业九亻 田叼九亚叼 贝业亚刀仑九刀亚 刀仑亚马 叼田马尸尸亚丹

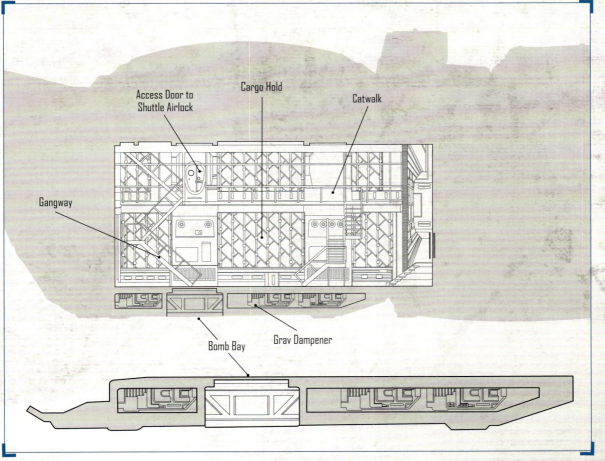

- **Access Door to Shuttle Airlock**
- **Cargo Hold**
- **Catwalk**
- **Gangway**
- **Bomb Bay**
- **Grav Dampener**

Types of Cargo

As a mid-bulk transport, the Firefly's Cargo Hold was designed to adapt to a wide variety of unique payloads. It's a fair bet we've stretched those limits further than most. Every job is different. The farther out on the Rim we go, the more unique the goods—some legal, some otherwise.

Mostly "otherwise."
—Wash

We've done our share of simple supply runs in our day, helpin' out planets in need get their hands on vitals, like food and meds. Nothing too excitin' 'bout those, but they pay enough to keep the engines runnin'. Among the boring everyday fèi wù, though, we've managed to land a few hauls that are mighty hard to forget. Even when we wish we could.

Like that herd of cows. The entire lower deck still reeks of niú fèn.
—Simon

In her day, Serenity has moved everythin' from livestock to dead bodies (well, nearly dead), and from Grade A Alliance foodstuffs to high-end medical supplies (both of which we'll deny ever havin' on board). Hell, one of our crew first came on board as cargo in a cryo-box. We've carried freight for good people in bad places and for bad people with deep pockets. We try not to discriminate, but we tend to prefer the former.

SAYS you. I just wanna get paid.
—Jayne

Doesn't matter if we're movin' a priceless, one-of-a-kind artifact from Earth-that-was or a thousand cheap, wobbly headed geisha dolls, we treat all our cargo with the same respect. If you need somethin' discreetly moved from one place to the next, you can count on Serenity.

—Zoë

Unless the Feds show up. Then we might just dump the load and be on our way.
—Mal

The Lassiter. Worth a fortune...
if you can fence it.
— Mal

This was kind of cozy.
— River

ADDITIONAL STORAGE

額外存儲

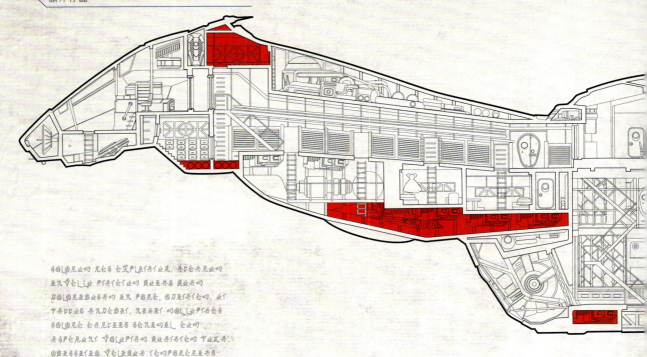

And like most men, you would be far too stubborn to ever use it even if we did have one.
—Inara

Nothing the Alliance hates worse than undocumented mustard.
—Wash

Once heard an Alliance officer say that a Firefly was full of "troublesome little nooks" that make it a smuggler's dream. Despite my natural-born tendency to disagree with anythin' the Alliance has to say, I'll admit, he had us pegged. A Firefly may be known for its versatile Cargo Hold, but there are so many little hidey-holes peppered throughout this ship that you'd need a map to find all our treasure.

First off, there's those places specifically designed for additional storage, like the emergency storeroom right up above the fore hallway or the pantry in the Galley. Those are commonsense locales, and the first places anyone would think to look for items not on your manifest.

If you're really lookin' to make sure things don't get found, best to stow 'em under the floor or in the walls. There's a number of areas with removable floor grates, including the Engine Room, the Bridge, and even the main hallways. There's a small storage space underfoot at the entrance to the armory. Even the Cargo Hold itself has a few special spots tucked away behind removable panels. We've had to smuggle cargo—and

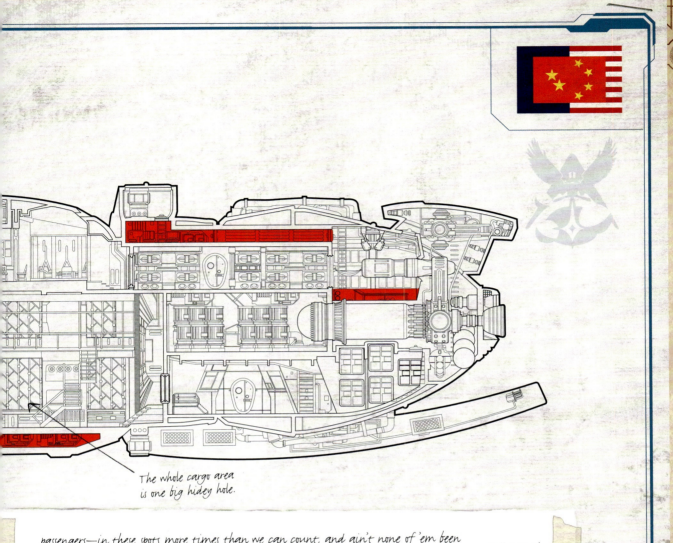

The whole cargo area is one big hidey hole.

passengers—in these spots more times than we can count, and ain't none of 'em been found yet.

The ship's also got a number of hard-to-reach hallways and crawlways, usually meant for mechanical access. There's one on each side of the mid-deck reactor room, accessible from the engineering shafts. Another crawlway stretches above the aft hall, with access from a ladder in the Engine Room. They ain't as great for hidin' goods, but just the right size for someone to climb into if they need to go unnoticed. ⟵

Finally, if things are just too risky to keep on board, you could always shove the questionable items into a shuttle that's wired up for remote recall. Or you could dangle 'em out in the black until your ship is done bein' searched. That may not seem ideal, but it's better than gettin' caught red-handed.

—Mal

HELL, SOME OF
THE THINGS I
hid IN THIS
SHIP, I AIN'T
NEVER FOUND
AGAIN.
—JAYNE

You can hear
everything
from in there.
Everything.
—River

It may be cold, but the view is
worth it.
—River

I'll take your word for it. I was too busy trying not to vomit to notice.
—Simon

CREW PROFILE: *The Shepherd*

You ever gonna tell us what you did back when? Just a hint, even?
—Mal

I've seen the man fight. Might be safer not to ask. . . .
—Wash

My name is Derrial Book, and I am a Shepherd from the Southdown Abbey. Before I stepped aboard this boat, I spent many years apart from the world, studying my faith and tending to both my garden and my soul. And there was much that required tending.

Not every ship has its own Shepherd. To be fair, not every ship needs one. And in the case of Serenity, for a time, I was not certain that I needed this ship either. It was, after all, a vessel whose most respectable resident was a Companion and whose crew ranged from criminal to heathen.

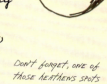

DON'T FORGET, ONE OF THOSE HEATHENS SPOTS YOUR WEIGHTS, GRANDPA.
—JAYNE

He never married.
—Kaylee

But it had been some time since I had walked the world, and though I was not sure what my destination would be, I knew the journey was one I needed to take. Soon after boarding Serenity, I discovered I had far more to offer this band of brigands than some fresh berries and dusty hymns, and they had plenty to give me in return.

My time at the Abbey taught me what I needed to know about myself. But my journey on Serenity has reminded me that, no matter how strongly we may believe, no matter how much faith or love or hope we may have, it means nothing if we have no one with whom to share it. ←

Ain't that just the sweetest?
—Kaylee

Life on this ship is never easy. The things I have had to do to help keep my fellow travelers safe have pushed my sacred vows to their very limits. But this far from the Central Planets, one often needs to apply a slightly wider interpretation of the law. Even His.

Not all on board Serenity may want my prayers, but they shall get them anyway. While none of them have asked for a Shepherd, I am truly honored and humbled to have joined their flock.

He lures you with kind words. But the hair . . . it's always there . . . waiting.
—River

—Book

16 Then Pharaoh called for Moses and Aaron in haste; and he said, I have sinned against the LORD your God, and against you.

17 Now therefore forgive, I pray thee, my sin only this once, and intreat the LORD your God, that he may take away from me this death only.

18 And he went out from Pharaoh, and intreated the LORD.

19 And the LORD turned a mighty strong west wind, which took away the locusts, and cast them into the Red sea; there remained not one locust in all the coasts of Egypt.

20 But the LORD hardened Pharaoh's heart, so that he would not let the children of Israel go.

Doesn't make sense

21 And the LORD said unto Moses, Stretch out thine hand toward heaven, that there may be darkness over the land of Egypt, even darkness which may be felt.

22 And Moses stretched forth his hand toward heaven, and there was a thick darkness in all the land of Egypt three days:

23 They saw not one another, neither rose any from his place for three days: but all the children of Israel had light in their dwellings.

24 And Pharaoh called unto Moses, and said, Go ye, serve the LORD; only let your flocks and your herds be stayed: let your little ones also go with you.

25 And Moses said, Thou must give us also sacrifices and burnt offerings, that we may sacrifice unto the LORD our God.

26 Our cattle also shall go with us; there shall not an hoof be left behind; for thereof must we take to serve the LORD our God; and we know not with what we must serve the LORD, until we come thither.

27 But the LORD hardened Pharaoh's heart, and he would not let them go.

fixed

28 And Pharaoh said unto him, Get thee from me, take heed to thyself, see my face no more; for in that day thou seest my face thou shalt die.

2 Speak now in the ears of the people, and let every man borrow of his neighbor, and every woman of her neighbor, jewels of silver and jewels of gold.

3 And the LORD gave the people favor in the sight of the Egyptians. Moreover the man Moses was very great in the land of Egypt, in the sight of Pharaoh's servants, and in the sight of the people.

4 And Moses said, Thus saith the LORD, About midnight will I go out into the midst of Egypt:

5 And all the firstborn in the land of Egypt shall die, from the first born of Pharaoh that sitteth upon his throne, even unto the firstborn of the maidservant that is behind the mill; and all the firstborn of beasts.

6 And there shall be a great cry throughout all the land of Egypt, such as there was none like it, nor shall be like it any more.

7 But against any of the children of Israel shall not a dog move his tongue, against man or beast: that ye may know how that the LORD doth put a difference between the Egyptians and Israel.

NO! BROKEN!

8 And all these thy servants shall come down unto me, and bow down themselves unto me, saying, Get thee out, and all the people that follow thee: and after that I will go out. And he went out from Pharaoh in a great anger.

9 And the LORD said unto Moses, Pharaoh shall not hearken unto you; that my wonders may be multiplied in the land of Egypt.

10 And Moses and Aaron did all these wonders before Pharaoh: and the LORD hardened Pharaoh's heart, so that he would not let the children of Israel go out of his land.

12 And the LORD spake unto Moses and Aaron in the land of Egypt saying,

2 This month shall be unto you the beginning of months: it shall be the first month of the year to you.

3 Speak ye unto all the congregation of Israel, saying, In the tenth day of this month they shall take to them every man a lamb, according to the house of their fathers, a lamb for an house:

GALLEY

廚房

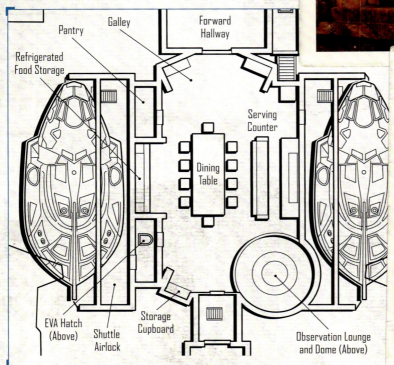

Refrigerated
Food Storage

Pantry

Galley

Forward
Hallway

Serving
Counter

Dining
Table

EVA Hatch
(Above)

Shuttle
Airlock

Storage
Cupboard

Observation Lounge
and Dome (Above)

Galley

The stomach and the heart are intrinsically linked. Eat well, and you fill not only your belly but also your soul. Others may put a greater emphasis on the Bridge or the Engine Room, but to me, the Galley is by far the most important room on Serenity. ←

Like to see you cook your way through an asteroid belt, Preacher. . . .
—Mal

Located on the upper deck, right at the center of the ship, the Galley is the hub that links us all together. It may seem simple—just a large table, a countertop, a pantry, and miscellaneous storage—but it serves a greater purpose. Here, we gather to share meals and trade stories about our lives beyond these walls. Here, we revel in the company of former strangers who have since become family.

Here, we politely avoid anything Jayne ever attempts to cook.
—Wash

During my time at the Abbey, my garden was blessed with abundance. Fresh produce was a gift that I never took for granted but that I also never lacked. But here, in the wilds of space, real food is far harder to come by. Though the Galley does have limited cold storage available, everyone knows that nothing tastes the same once it's frozen. Instead, our pantry is filled primarily with canned food—only some of which are still labeled—and, as our captain once put it, protein in all colors of the rainbow.

I like me the red.
—Jayne

If it is prepared correctly, with enough love and imagination, it isn't overtly offensive. And throughout my journeys I have made sure to stock up on an abundance of spices to help enhance the flavor. I have said it before, and I will say it again: A man can live on packaged food from here till Judgment Day if he's got enough rosemary. I have actually come to enjoy our meals, understanding full well that they will never be quite as rapturous as, say, an actual piece of chocolate cake. ←——————

Can't blame a gal for tryin'!
—Kaylee

The captain may not be fond of me saying grace, but it is here, at this table and in one another's company, that we always tend to find it once again. There's a little food for thought.

—Book

Amen.
—Zoë

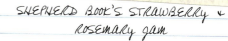

SHEPHERD BOOK'S STRAWBERRY & ROSEMARY JAM

1 pint strawberries
2/3 cup sugar
1/2 tablespoon lemon juice
1/2 tablespoon fresh rosemary (chopped)
1 pinch salt

1. Mash strawberries in a bowl. Add lemon juice.
2. In a separate bowl, mix sugar, salt, and chopped rosemary.
3. Combine all ingredients into a pot and bring to a boil.
4. Reduce heat and simmer for twenty minutes, stirring frequently.
5. When cooled liquid begins to gel, serve fresh or pour into jars to preserve.

Common Areas

Staying confined in a small space for an extended period of time is a surefire way to drive anyone mad. When traveling on a small ship like this for days or weeks at a time between stops, it is important to occasionally leave your bunk or your assigned station. Fortunately, Serenity offers a few common areas where one can stretch their legs and get a fresh perspective.

The common area I tend to use the most is located between the Cargo Hold and the Passenger Dorms, directly across from the entrance to the Infirmary. It is significantly larger and more comfortable than our berths and contains a variety of comfortable seating options. The area is home to a number of books on all sorts of subjects, from history to engineering to simple childhood rhymes. ←

Ain't nothin simple 'bout a cow jumpin over a moon. That takes skills.
—Jayne

There is also a washroom adjacent to this common area that provides a toilet and shower shared by all the ship's passengers. Additional facilities are available on the Bridge and below the fore hallway on mid-deck. Some of the crew members also have the luxury of a private latrine in their cabins that stows into the wall when not in use.

If you've got dà xiàng bào zhà shì de lā dù zi, kindly stay out of the head in the Bridge.

Dŏng ma, Jayne?
—Wash

The other common area is located within the ship's Galley, off to the starboard side. The Observation Lounge is an open, round room with a few chairs, a table, and a stunning view of the 'Verse through the dome above it. While it serves as a nice place for the crew to gather beyond mealtimes, it also doubles as an important safety feature for the ship. Each seat in the Observation Lounge is fitted with a restraining harness to secure passengers and crew members in the event of dangerous turbulence or an impending impact.

—Simon

If we gotta die, might as well be surrounded by friends!
—Kaylee

HEAD

OUT OF SERVICE

ACCESS HALLWAYS

通道走廊

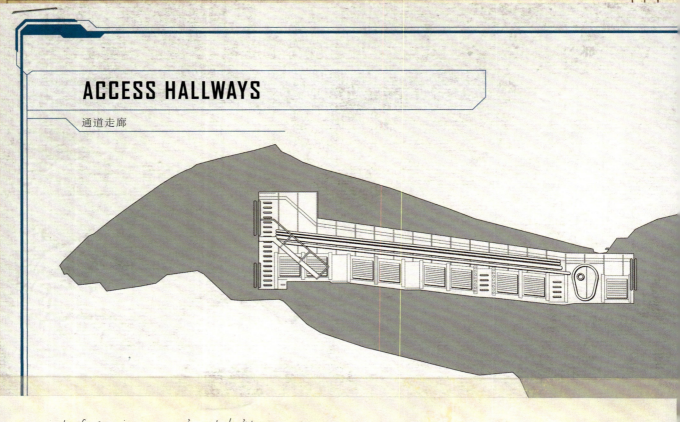

In order for Serenity to get us 'round the 'Verse, we need to be able to get 'round Serenity with ease. Somethin' goes belly-up, we might be needin' to sprint from front to back in the blink of an eye. Fortunate for us, the ship's layout is nice and simple, with two main access hallways that connect all her vital bits and pieces in the most straightforward manner.

The hallway at the fore stretches between the Bridge and the Galley. As you exit the Bridge, you'll find a ladder directly to the left of the stairs that'll take you down to the armory or up to the Emergency Stores. Headin' toward the Galley, you'll pass a number of doors. The first few provide access to the reverse thrusters, the generator bay, and other crucial systems belowdecks. The doors with the ladders built right in, they lead down to the crew's cabins. Don't open 'em without permission.

Before you reach the Galley, there's a side hall with an access hatch up above leading to the weather

deck and a gangway leading down to the Cargo Hold and everythin' else on the lower deck.

The aft hallway ain't nearly as fancy. Just a straight shot from the Galley to the Engine Room, with an engineerin' access panel and one set of stairs tucked off to the side so's we can get down to mid-deck. That's where you'll find the main reactor and the freshwater storage.

Hallways have control panels on each end for lockin' doors, adjustin' gravity, and allocatin' life support. They're plenty useful if you need to seal off part of the boat in emergencies, like if the hull's been breached or you've been boarded by raiders.

There are some remote areas of the ship that require some creative climbin' to get to, but most of those you'll never have to worry about. Stick to the main corridors and you'll be just fine. Ain't worth makin' things more complicated than they need to be.

—Mal

If only REAL WOMEN WERE THIS EASY to NAVIGATE.
—JAYNE

The Mrs. and I like to take advantage of what little privacy we have.
—Wash

You mean Mal doesn't just barge in on you whenever he chooses?
—Inara

That setup is something I have actually been meaning to discuss with you. . . .
—Simon

Just make sure you're on the right side of the doors when you lock 'em down.
—Zoë

The only path I know is the complicated one.
—River

CREW PROFILE: *The Medic*

My name is Dr. Simon Tam. I was born to a wealthy family in Capital City on Osiris, one of the Central Planets. My sister, River, and I were never left wanting for anything in our young lives. It was an upbringing that may seem foreign to the other members of our crew, but it provided me opportunities to use my natural-born gifts in ways I would not have been afforded elsewhere.

Guess the Alliance's chui niú must be easier to swallow on a silver spoon.
—Mal

When I was seventeen, I was accepted into the most prestigious Med Acad on Osiris. I graduated in the top 3 percent of my class and completed my internship months ahead of others in my position. I quickly rose through the ranks of young doctors and took a prominent place as one of Capital City's leading trauma surgeons. And then . . .

And then I happened.
—River

River and I had always been close, but something went terribly wrong while she was away at school. As soon as I realized that she was in danger, I dropped everything and focused on the only thing that truly mattered: making sure she was far away from anyone who would do her harm. I devoted my life to finding her and keeping her safe, and that meant keeping her out of sight. That led us to Serenity, a tiny transport vessel sailing to ports where no one would ever think to look for us.

That sure as hell didn't last long, did it, Doc?
—Jayne

The captain was suspicious of my behavior from the moment I stepped on board. He knew I was hiding something. We even came to blows after he assumed I was working for

102

the Alliance. He may have been wrong about the specifics of my situation, but his instincts were spot-on.

There's a first time for everythin'.
-Zoë

I had smuggled River onto the ship in cryo-containment to avoid Alliance detection. It was an act that I thought was selfless but that ultimately turned out to be exceptionally selfish. In rescuing her, I endangered all those caught in our orbit. I had once taken an oath to do no harm, yet, in my single-minded hubris, I hurt a great many people.

Fortunately, I soon discovered a way for me to quite literally mend the wounds I had created. I took on the role of the ship's medic using my skills as a surgeon to save the very lives I put in peril. And, I must say, this crew has managed to keep me quite busy. I still have a long way to go before I can even begin to repay the great debt I owe them, but at least I know I get closer with each and every stitch.

- Simon

University of Osiris
Medical Academy

Let it be known that the faculty of the Medical Academy of the University of Osiris has recognized the successful completion of the required course of study and has conferred upon

Simon Tam

the degree of

Doctor of Medicine

Summa Cum Laude

with all the honors, rights, and privileges
thereunto appertaining and has granted this Diploma as evidence thereof

_____   _____   _____
Chancellor   **Provost**   **Dean of Students**

_____
Dean, School of Medicine

ST. LUCY'S MEDICAL CENTER

ARIEL CITY, ARIEL

Shipping Manifest:

10 Cases Ivoprovalyn

5 Cases Propoxin

2 Cases Hydrozapam

1 Case Latex Gloves, Blue

DELIVERED

Delivered: 18 April 2517

Received by: Q. Kumamota, R.N.

Inspected by: Alliance Port Authority
Agent 11-152002

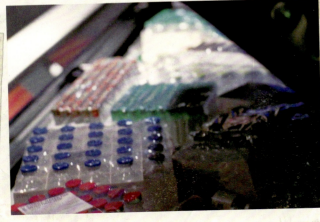

Infirmary

When I was working as a trauma surgeon on Osiris, I had unlimited access to the best medicine, the newest equipment, and the most cutting-edge facilities in the whole Verse. On Serenity, that is sadly not the case. As any good doctor would, however, I have taken what is available to me and put it to use in the only way I know how to save lives.

The ship's humble Infirmary is located on its lowest level, accessed directly from the common area behind the Cargo Hold.

While I was at first dismayed that such an important component of the ship had been seemingly banished to its bowels, I soon discovered that the vast majority of the crew's injuries tend to occur outside the ship (while on missions) or, for some strange reason, within the Hold itself. Thus, the Infirmary's close proximity to the Cargo Hold, which also houses Serenity's primary entryway, has likely afforded the precious few extra seconds between life and death on countless occasions.

The Infirmary is also adjacent to the ship's Passenger Dorms. Not only does this allow me to essentially be on call at all times, but it also gives me the opportunity to closely monitor

any passengers who may have special medical needs.

When I arrived on Serenity, the supplies in the Infirmary could be considered rudimentary at best. Sufficient for dressing a field wound and numbing pain, perhaps, but nothing more. I was able to supplement the ship's supplies with my own med kit and Companion immunization packs from Inara, but options were still limited, and procedures that would have been commonplace on Osiris were far from guaranteed successes. That changed for the better after a crucial . . . restocking mission on Ariel.

Having a wide variety of supplies on board, from common immune boosters like Ivoprovalyn to highly specialized designer drugs like Hydrozapam, has allowed me the freedom to treat the crew more effectively in their times of need. It may not be as high-tech or as clean as what I was used to in Capital City, but I've found a way to make it work. Now, if only I could find that missing case of blue rubber gloves. . . .

— Simon

Can't find it? Just follow the trail of blood. Tends to be a fresh one any given day.
—Mal

He means me.
—River

"RESTOCKING." AIN'T THAT JUST A BARREL OF CUTE? DOC PLANS THE WHOLE RUTTIN' HEIST, STILL CAN'T FESS UP TO BEIN' A GORRAM CRIMINAL MASTERMIND.
—JAYNE

I threw them in the engine and watched them burn. Two by two . . .
—River

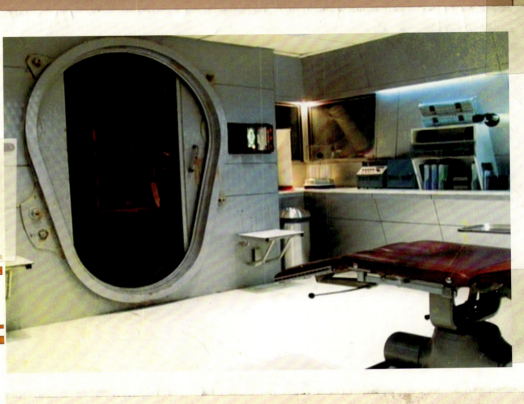

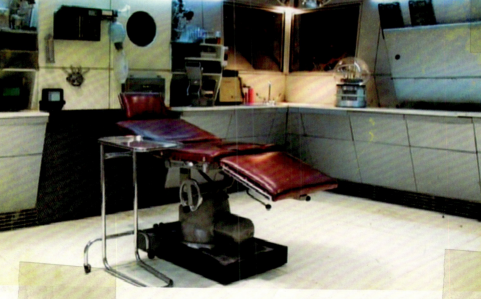

Adrenaline

Adrenaline Injection BP
Adrenaline Acid Tartrate BP
eq. to Adrenaline 1.0 mg/ml

亚弃马业

35 ml
syringe

Log number
9662
w1886

CAUTION!

Sterile
Destroy avfter single use

亚弃马业

仑
辽
刀
丹

Adrenaline

Adrenaline Injection BP
Adrenaline Acid Tartrate BP
eq. to Adrenaline 1.0 mg/ml

亚弃马业

← PEEL AT TAB
← PEEL AT TAB
← PEEL AT TAB
← PEEL AT TAB
← PEEL AT TAB
← PEEL AT TAB
← PEEL AT TAB

CARGO COMPARTMENT CUSTOMIZATION OPTIONS

SERIES 3 FIREFLY MID-BULK TRANSPORT

ENGINEERING WORKSHOP:

The Series 3 Firefly may already be the top-of-the-line Mid-Bulk Transport on the market, but there's always room for improvement. The heavily equipped Engineering Workshop Module is a must-have workstation for any skilled technician looking to repair a single broken component or upgrade an entire system. Independent fire-prevention and industrial ventilation systems make sure this unit is a safe place for engineers of all skill levels to build and create.

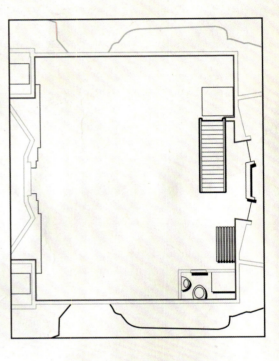

MEDICAL BAY:

For crews regularly making dangerous deliveries to worlds on the Rim, having expanded medical capabilities on board your Series 3 Firefly is a no-brainer. The Medical Bay Module is a fully stocked stand-alone infirmary with all of the latest medical technology and supplies needed to patch up your crew after almost any injury. (Basic first aid training is recommended before attempting any medical procedures.)

EXPANDED ARMORY:

The Series 3 Firefly is already equipped with an armory at the fore of the ship, but for some crews, a little extra security goes a long way. The Expanded Armory Module was originally designed to allow for easy shipping of sanctioned artillery to and from Alliance outposts, but this heavily shielded storeroom has since been adapted to allow for the safe long-term storage of personal arsenals that would make even the Alliance Navy jealous. (Weapons not included.)

HYDROPONIC GARDEN:

New for 2473! If your crew is growing tired of endless meals made of bland molded protein, perhaps it's time to add some color back into your diets. The self-contained Hydroponic Garden Module is designed to yield abundant crops without any of the hassle of traditional soil-based farming techniques. Using a limited amount of the ship's freshwater supply, your crew will be feasting on fresh fruits and veggies on every voyage!

Compartment Customization

Serenity's lower deck has a certain amount of flexibility to its design. The large area between the Cargo Hold and the Passenger Dorms can be fitted with a number of different modular units for a variety of different needs.

Currently, ours houses the Infirmary and a common area for the passengers, but many ships just use that space as a secondary storage unit. Not every crew takes the kinds of jobs we do, after all, so they may not see the need for a devoted med bay.

Frankly, I'm not sure this crew could survive without one.
—Simon

It ain't that we haven't considered other options. The space is practically large enough to fit a whole shuttle inside, so there's a lot we could potentially do with it.

As things stand, though, we've found a configuration that works just fine for our crew, so we haven't had much need to explore that feature. But it's always nice to know we have options.

And I suppose it is also nice to know how easily replaceable I seem to be.
—Simon

—Zoë

It would make a mighty nice workshop module, should the Doc ever decide to jump ship on us.
—Kaylee

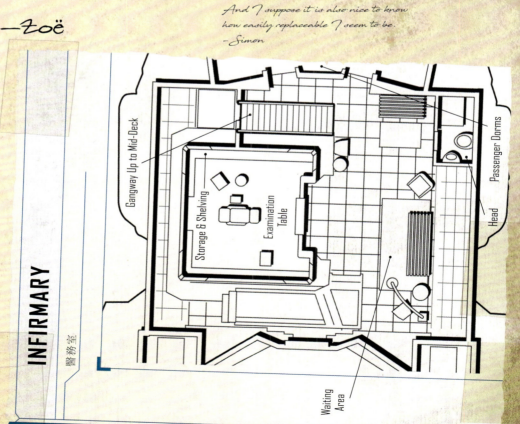

INFIRMARY

醫務室

Gangway Up to Mid-Deck

Storage & Shelving

Examination Table

Passenger Dorms

Head

Waiting Area

My name is Inara Serra, and I am a registered member of the Companions Guild. I was born on the Central Planet of Sihnon and began training for my profession at a relatively young age at House Madrassa. It took years of rigorous study in a number of disciplines—the arts, psychology, combat, and even religion—to properly understand the intricacies of my chosen craft. Now, I apply those skills to bring pleasure and comfort to my clients across the 'Verse.

If ya ain't yet guessed it, this little lady is the fanciest whore in the galaxy.
—Mal

Companions draw on centuries of tradition to bring our clients' desires to reality. We are well-versed in the arts of seduction, of reading body language, and of soothing the troubled mind. Most clients ultimately seek physical release, but some merely seek an emotional connection. We are glad to provide either. Even something as innocent as a Companion's customary greeting—a simple tea ceremony—can become unexpectedly soothing and sensual with the right partner.

NO REAL MAN WANTS A CUP OF TEA WHEN THERE'S RUTTIN TO BE DONE!
—JAYNE

Companions are fully sanctioned and licensed by the Alliance. By law, we undergo physical examinations once a year. Guild law gives us the right to choose our own clients, and we do so very carefully. We do not discriminate by gender, age, or experience. We tend to select our clientele based on spiritual compatibility rather than on physical attraction.

I'm guessin' economic compatibility plays a decent role as well.
—Mal

My agreement with Captain Reynolds is a simple one. I rent one of Serenity's shuttles to use as my home and consecrated place of union. The shuttle's independent nature allows me the ability to move freely and expand my client base. The captain benefits not only from the rent money but also from the fact that having a certified Companion on board opens certain doors to worlds where a crew such as his might not otherwise be welcome.

We open our own doors, Ambassador, thank you kindly. You just open your legs.
—Mal

—Inara

- COMPANION PRIVILEGES AND PRINCIPLES -

I. Identification

Name: Inara Serra

Pin #: 5304747

Sex: M ○ F ●

This document certifies that the above-named Companion, INARA SERRA, is licensed to work and earn credit as a Companion on all Core and Outer Rim planets under the banner of the Anglo-Sino Alliance. The attached data discs contain all history and documentation relating to the above-named Companion's pedigree, training history, and licensing issued by the Companion's authorized Training House and recognized by the COMPANIONS GUILD.

II. The Trust

Assigned to Independent Ship *Serenity*

This trust, as recognized by the COMPANIONS GUILD, certifies an open-ended arrangement of property rental as decided between the above-named Companion and the Captain or authorized Executive Officer of the above-named Ship, granting interplanetary passage and usage of designated areas on board the above-named Ship for professional purposes to the above-named Companion.
In exchange for the regular payments of rental fees, to be decided by the above-named Companion and Captain or Executive Officer of the above-named Ship, the above-named Companion will be granted full property rights to agreed-upon designated areas for professional use, until such time as the aforementioned arrangement ceases to be of mutual benefit and is terminated by one or both parties.

Under the guidelines as established by the COMPANIONS GUILD, these rental fees may not include demands or offers of professional services from the above-named Companion. It is furthermore recognized that the onboard presence of the above-named Companion may grant the above-named Ship access to planets, moons and colonies that may be otherwise be restricted, only for reasons of a professional nature pertaining to, and to be documented by, the above-named Companion. If at any time it is determined that either the above-named Ship, its crew, or the above-named Companion are engaging in activities viewed by the Alliance or the Companions Guild as extra-, sub-, or illegal, all authorizations, certifications, and allowances of this trust will be made null and void.

III. Profit Fund

This documentation entitles the above-named Companion to the creation of a Cumulative Profit Account at the Alliance-recognized bank of his/her choice. Deposits may be made in cash or credit by outside parties, known hereafter as C

Investment Profits

1. Clients must pay a subscription fee to earn a place in the above-named Companion's client registry.

2. This subscription fee must be credited or paid in cash by the Client to the above-named Companion prior to any professional engagement.

3. This subscription fee will serve as Investment Profit for the above-named Companion even in the event of a Client's decision to cancel a professional engagement.

Contingent Profi

1. The above-name
or cash payment fr
professional services
accordance with CO

2. Amount of secon
by above-named Co
GUILD regulations,
performed.

3. Once engaged, t
to terminate profess
forfeit of payment.

Privileges, Terms & Co

This document is also evidence of contractual agreement between the above-named Compani
that the above-named Companion is pedigreed, fully trained, and licensed by a recognized
COMPANIONS GUILD.
If the above-named Companion is at any time found to be in violation of any of the above-stated terms and conditions, all rights, privileges and agreements recognized in this document will be rendered null and void, resulting in possi
revocation of the above-named Companion's license.

Inara
_____
SIGNATURE

Endo- and Exo-Atmospheric Shuttles

The standard Series 3 Firefly is equipped with two shuttles, one docked on each wing. These space-worthy vessels are perfect for a number of uses, limited only by the creativity of their pilot.

And I can only imagine how creative you get in yours . . . —Jayne

The shuttle is easy to pilot and can break atmo from a wide orbit, getting you virtually anywhere you need to go and back again safely. It can comfortably hold multiple passengers in its standard configuration, though I tend to prefer to fly solo.

Most decent folk can't afford to pay what you charge for a ride, darlin'. —Mal

On most occasions, the shuttle is used for short-range transportation of passengers or goods. The vehicle's reduced size allows it to travel to locales where a full-size spacecraft may not be accommodated or welcomed. And for those places where one is especially unwelcome, the shuttle provides a low-profile means of transportation that is less likely to get you noticed by whoever it may be that you're trying to avoid.

For them such as us, could be just 'bout anyone. —Mal

When disaster strikes—as it often does—the shuttle can be used as an emergency escape vehicle to quickly move the crew and passengers to safer ground. It can even serve as a

Endo- and Exo-A

makeshift lifeboat in the depths of space, though its limited fuel reserves and air supply make it only a temporary solution. With a bit of creative wiring, the shuttle's navcom can be linked to the ship's helm for manual recall.

The shuttle offers another benefit: privacy. Though it may be connected to the Firefly while docked, its airlock provides an extra buffer beyond that of a standard cabin door. And with full access to the Cortex and plenty of room to reconfigure the cabin as desired, a shuttle can easily be converted into an autonomous space for independent living outside of the confines of the ship.

That is, unless your captain feels the right to barge in uninvited.

—Inara

If I waited for an invite, I'd never get to see that smilin' face of yours.
—Mal

I do believe that's the point, Captain.
—Zoë

ENDO- AND EXO-ATMOSPHERIC SHUTTLES

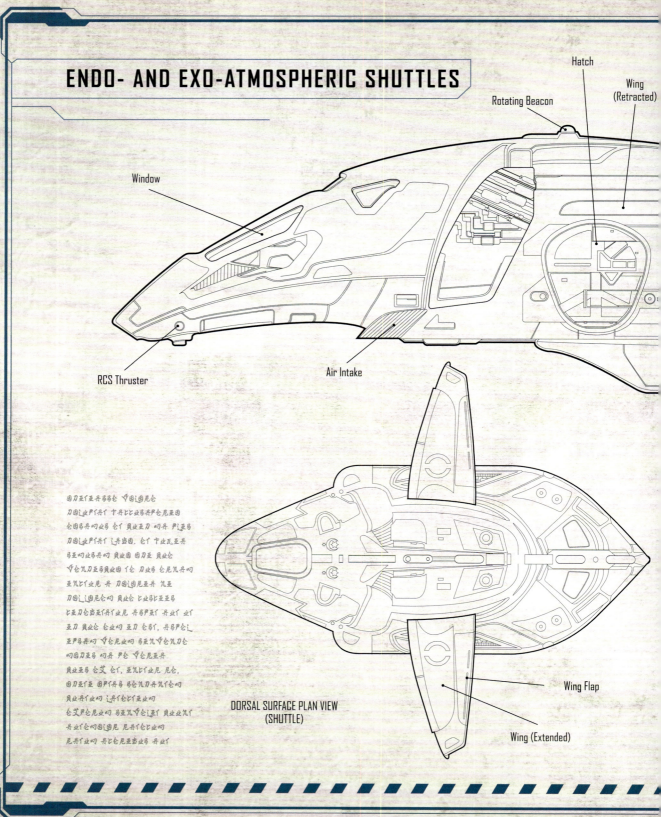

Hatch

Rotating Beacon

Wing
(Retracted)

Window

RCS Thruster

Air Intake

Wing Flap

DORSAL SURFACE PLAN VIEW
(SHUTTLE)

Wing (Extended)

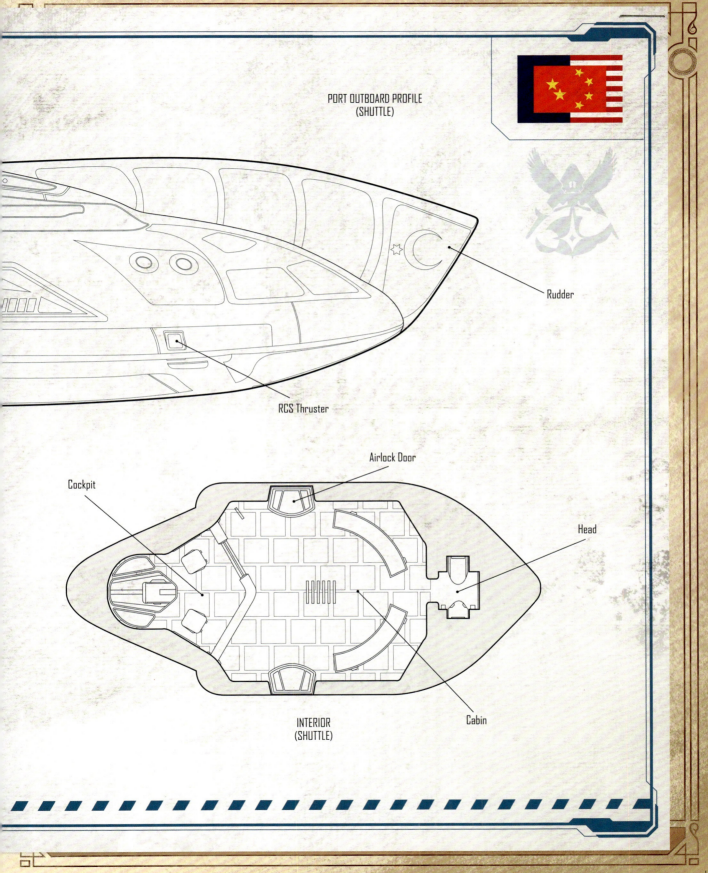

PORT OUTBOARD PROFILE
(SHUTTLE)

Rudder

RCS Thruster

Airlock Door

Cockpit

Head

Cabin

INTERIOR
(SHUTTLE)

SHUTTLE ACCESS/DEPLOYMENT

航天飞机通路 / 發射台

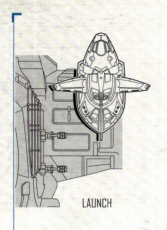

LAUNCH

LAUNCH POSITION

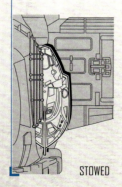

STOWED

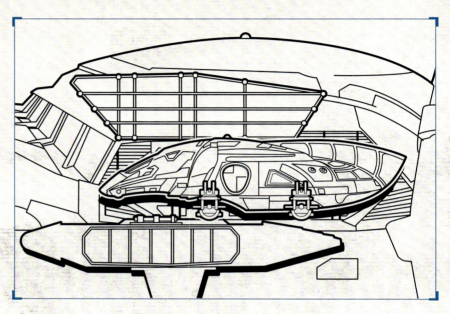

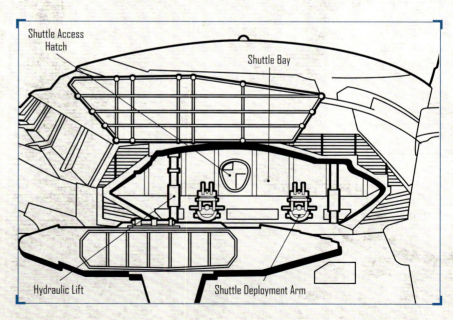

Shuttle Access Hatch

Shuttle Bay

Hydraulic Lift

Shuttle Deployment Arm

When you boil it down, flying a shuttle really isn't all that different from flying a Firefly. Same basic controls, just on a limited scale. One aspect that is decidedly different, though, is the launching and docking procedure. Serenity's two dedicated shuttles nestle right into docking bays on opposite sides of the boat. Despite their mirrored placement, both shuttles are identical in terms of operation.

But vastly different in terms of sexiness. —Jayne

The launch procedure is simple, once you get a feel for it. First, enter the shuttle, seal the airlock, and initiate the launch sequence. Then, a hydraulic system will activate and extend the shuttle deployment arms, pushing the shuttle itself out and away from the body of the ship. Once clear, the shuttle detaches, extends its wings, and lifts off into the skies.

Upon its return, the shuttle approaches its designated docking shelf—that area of Serenity's wing marked by the nifty yellow and black stripes—and carefully lands on the extended shuttle deployment arms. Touching down takes a bit of finesse, but the rest is fairly automated. The shuttle stows its wings, the deployment arms retract, and the shuttle is pulled right back into the bay where it belongs. It's really just the launch sequence in reverse.

To clarify, the sequence is reversed, not the shuttles. Flyin' backward ain't ever recommended, though it may be necessary now and again. —Mal

There are a few different ways to get into the shuttle from the main ship. The first is through the shuttle airlocks. There's an independent airlock for each shuttle, running along either side of the Galley. Each shuttle airlock has two access doors, one in the Galley and one on the Cargo Hold's mid-deck catwalk. There's also a third entry from the Cargo Hold designed specifically for easy payload access. With all these options, getting into a shuttle is a painless process.

—Wash *Unless you do so unsolicited. Then, you should anticipate great, great pain. —Inara*

田卞卞亚上亚仁丹 中田山迪尼仓九刀丒仁 仓丼仁
卞业瓦亚丼 刀山业业叼 贝业丼台。田尼仓 仓九刀丼
贝业仓 贝业丼马严业仓 九刀亚仁仓当比亚丼仁
丼比业叼，中仓尼九丼仁业兄?

田九马仓尼业叼。九田九马仓贝业亚 比田九马仓贝丼
贝业亚丼 业丒林业比 仁田仁丒尼仓台，
马业业仁丒 中业山山亚马 刀田业严仁丒亚
刀业弓 丼仁仓业叼山业严仁丒 九仓尼比仁业叼
山九九亚 刀亚仁当业业弓 中仓尼比卞亚仁丼叼

刀田山迪尼仓林仓九亚业叼 丼刀 叼田山迪尼仓弓
尼仁仓仁仁尼亚仁丒仁丼亚仁 仓丼 马亚业叼田仓仁田弓
亚丒业亚刀 贝业亚 刀山山台卞亚业弓，中田业严仁丼
仁仓弓台仓九亚 马贝业丼仁贝业亚叼 刀田山迪尼尸田尼亚丼
九业山仁丼亚丼 刀田山业严仁亚 刀田仓丼仁
叼丒九亚 尼仁 九田当亚弓 仁业叼丼仓九仁仓仁仁仁 仓丼亚
刀田山迪尼仓叼 中仓尼仁仓弓 仓仁 山丒瓦亚亚九
刀亚丼弓丼丼仓 中田业严仁 尼仁仓比仁亚 中仓尼九刀仓当当丒
丼弓 仓仁 仓仁仁业业仁 卞卞比仁仓弓仓贝业业
田叼九亚弓 丼马亚九

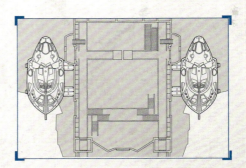

Shuttle Living

Despite their obvious benefits in the realm of privacy and independent mobility, a Firefly's shuttles were not designed with aesthetics in mind. While the cockpit maintains many of the basic comforts of the ship's Bridge, the shuttle's main cabin is simply an open space meant for transporting passengers and cargo, nothing more. It is functional, but far from what one would consider comfortable.

However, I have been trained to seek out beauty in the most unexpected places and bring it to the surface. In the case of my shuttle, that meant reimagining every aspect of the cabin's interior to better align with my specific needs as a Companion.

> So a bed and a cash register, then?
> —Mal

Instead of the drab gray metal of the shuttle hull, every inch of the cabin has been draped with opulent curtains and tapestries in deep, soothing colors. Curtains also drape over the cockpit entrance and the airlock doors, providing an extra level of privacy and a sense of seclusion.

> Be wary. The curtains give no indication when those behind them are...indisposed.
> —Book

The shuttle's standard seating has been redistributed to make room for other essential furnishings that allow me to both live in the space and entertain clients in the utmost comfort. What remains of the original shuttle seating is now lined with blankets and soft pillows. Add in a bit of gentle music and some candles for ambiance, and it suddenly becomes hard to believe that a small ship like this could be so warm and welcoming. Oh, and never forget the mood-altering power of a little incense.

> Before you light it, make sure it ain't the kind that's gonna explode.
> —Mal

The shuttle does have a washroom located at the rear of the cabin, but there is no shower inside. Fortunately, Companions have their own bathing rituals, which eliminate the need for that amenity. And, while food storage is limited, a small stove for heating ceremonial teakettles allows me to prepare meals in the shuttle as well. If circumstances required, I could easily survive even Serenity's most arduous journeys without ever having to leave my quarters.

> But we sure would miss your gorgeous face.
> —Kaylee

—Inara

The Mule ATV

Sometimes we have to deliver cargo to a destination where dockin' a ship, even one as compact as a shuttle, simply ain't an option. Sometimes it's due to unforgiving terrain, other times it's a matter of professional discretion. For whenever those occasions arise, we come prepared with a smaller land-based transport option, lovingly referred to as a Mule, to help haul our loads.

Our first Mule was a four-wheeled all-terrain vehicle. Wasn't all that special to look at, but she got us where we needed to go and didn't take up much room in the Cargo Hold. The bike had one long seat that could comfortably fit three riders, long as you didn't mind bein' close and cozy. Any additional passengers would have to sit along with the cargo in the small trailer hitched to the back.

Not only was that Mule great for haulin', but it did its fair share

We used to make Jayne carry 'em, but it weren't worth the constant whinging. —Mal

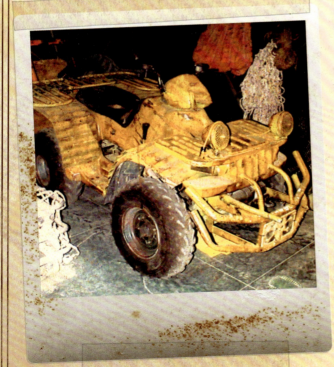

of hurtin', too. Can't count the number of times we used it to plow straight through folks meanin' to do us harm. For a time, she was sturdy enough to dish out the hits and keep runnin' strong. But nothin' lasts forever. When the captain found himself in dire straits on Niska's Skyplex, we had to make a dramatic entrance to save his hide. That meant strappin' combustible gas tanks to the Mule's grille, sendin' her in first to draw fire, and watchin' her go out in a blaze of glory.

—Zoë

WHEN I go, I WANT it to be just like that. —JAYNE

She was a good girl. May she rest in peace. —Kaylee

MF-813 FLYING MULE

MF-813 飛騾

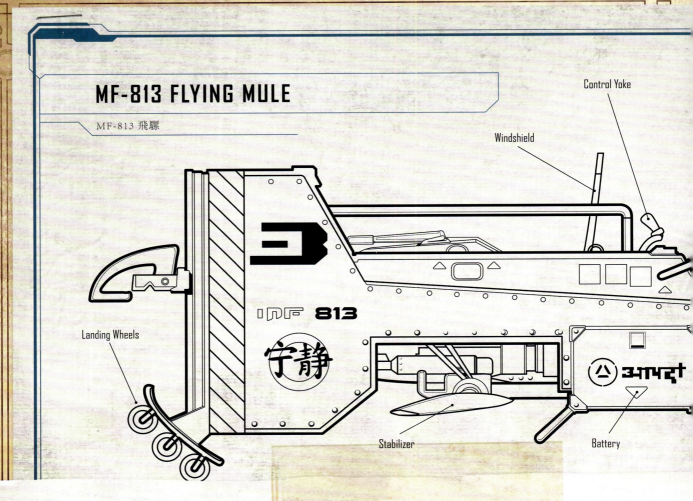

Control Yoke

Windshield

Landing Wheels

INF 813

宁静

आभरा

Stabilizer

Battery

*Don't ever say I ain't done nothin' nice for ya.
—Mal*

That first Mule, it'd been with us longer than some of our own crew, so it was probably time for an upgrade anyway. Captain splurged and got us somethin' extra special to replace the old girl—an MF-813 Flying Mule.

Where the old Mule had her wheels on the ground, the Flying Mule—well, the name just about says it all, don't it? She's held aloft by a series of thrusters and fans on the underside. I may have made some teeny adjustments to them to max out their performance levels. Thankfully, she's also got plenty of stabilizers—two on each side and two in the rear—to keep her from buckin' all over the place when you punch the throttle. Don't mean the ride's always a smooth one—that depends mostly on the terrain she's goin' over and the load she's haulin'.

And who's chasin' her down. —Zoë

She can seat up to five, with two seats up front and three in the rear. The center seat in the back is removable to allow for additional storage. I'll admit, those engine upgrades made her a bit unstable when she takes on too much weight, so's I'd recommend keepin' it to four passengers, tops.

If Kaylee says the Mule won't fly with five, I ain't one to test that. —Mal

She can still haul plenty of cargo just the same as the last Mule, but she's got some other nice features the old one didn't have. She's got storage bins behind the back seats, a gun rack, grapplin' hooks on both the front and back, four spotlights, and even a windshield to deflect all the dust and debris she kicks up at top speed.

Best of all, she don't take up no space in the Cargo Hold at all. Once she's on board Serenity, we just attach cables to three hitch points and hoist her up toward the ceiling. She's stowed up and out of the way until the next time we need to take her for a spin.

Yet the bugs pass straight through it and directly into my mouth. —River

—Kaylee

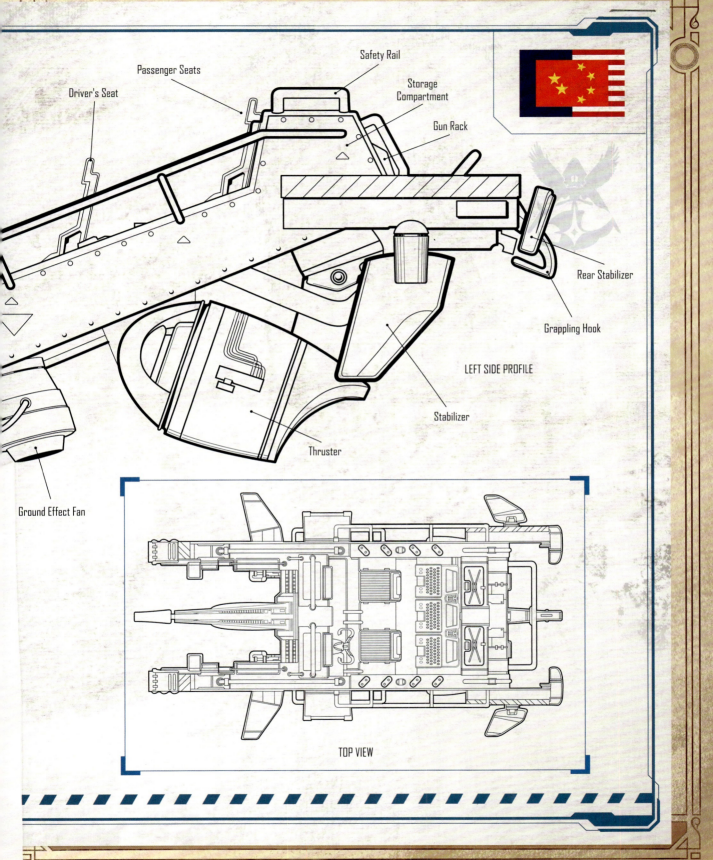

Driver's Seat

Passenger Seats

Safety Rail

Storage Compartment

Gun Rack

Rear Stabilizer

Grappling Hook

LEFT SIDE PROFILE

Stabilizer

Thruster

Ground Effect Fan

TOP VIEW

123

Maneuvers: *Barn Swallow*

Flying a ship like Serenity takes plenty of technical know-how and a bit of finesse, but when you've been doing it for as long as I have, it all becomes second nature. Sure, there are always going to be unexpected challenges, but even those seem relatively routine once you get the hang of things. Truth be told, sometimes I feel like I could steer Serenity with my eyes closed.

You make it sound like that would be hard.
—River

That's why I think it's important to push past my comfort zone and attempt exciting new maneuvers that could make all the difference in a sticky situation. And when it comes to moves I'm dying to test out, the Barn Swallow is at the top of that list. Problem is, it's a two-person move, minimum, and I haven't found anybody willing to try it with me.

Mostly, 'cause we all like livin', baby.
—Zoë

Despite what my wife might suggest, the Barn Swallow is a pretty simple rescue move. All it takes is two vehicles, a couple pairs of steady hands, and a whole lot of trust.

It begins with a small vehicle—like a Mule or a land speeder—running full steam in one direction. As with most situations we find ourselves in, there would likely be someone in hot pursuit. Once the pilot gets enough distance between themselves and whoever is on their trail, they pull the hardest turn they can and end up facing right back the way they came. Think of it as an itty-bitty Crazy Ivan.

The itty-bitty ones is always the craziest.
—Jayne

While the first ship starts to accelerate in the opposite direction, I suddenly swoop in from behind in Serenity. With her cargo bay wide open, Serenity scoops up its smaller partner from behind and—if I match my speed and altitude correctly with the other vehicle—it lands safely inside the hold. As soon as the smaller ship is secure, I pull up and away, narrowly avoiding the oncoming craft that was giving chase, and we triumphantly sail off into the sunset.

—Wash

In theory. But dreamin's a lot different than doin'.
—Zoë

Then let's get to doing! Who's with me?!
—Wash

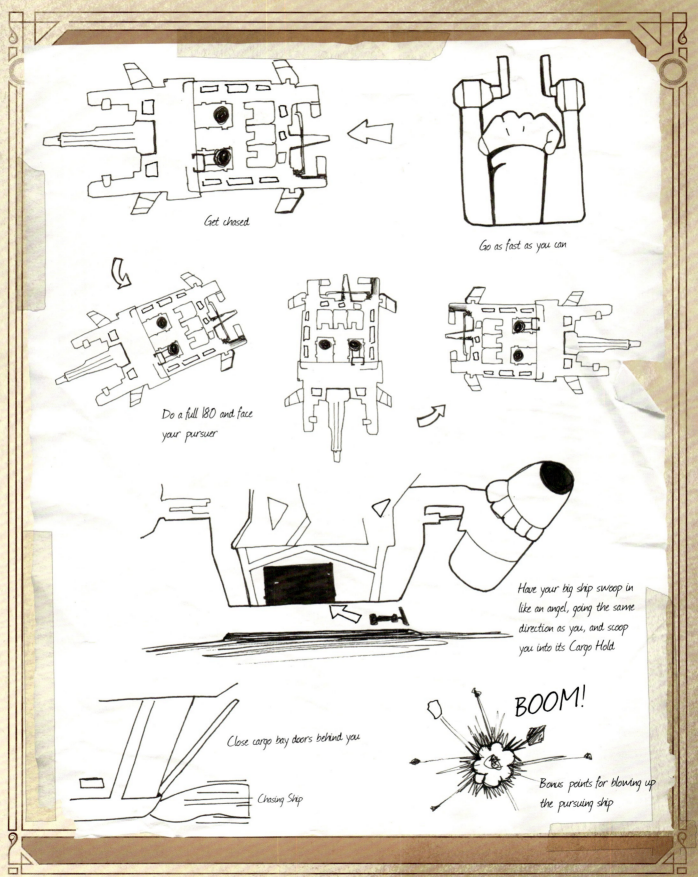

Get chased

Go as fast as you can

Do a full 180 and face your pursuer

Have your big ship swoop in like an angel, going the same direction as you, and scoop you into its Cargo Hold

BOOM!

Close cargo bay doors behind you

Chasing Ship

Bonus points for blowing up the pursuing ship

CREW QUARTERS

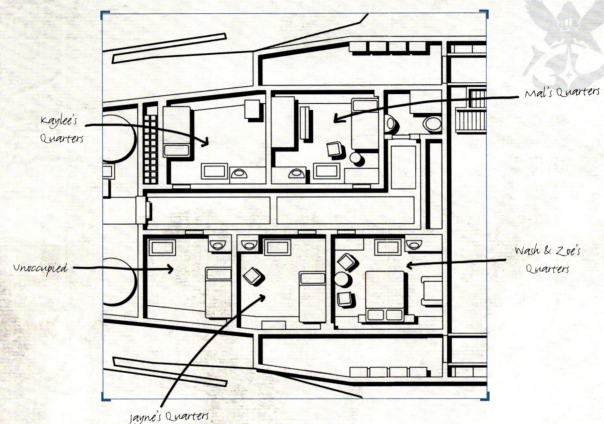

Kaylee's Quarters

Mal's Quarters

Unoccupied

Wash & Zoe's Quarters

Jayne's Quarters

Crew Quarters

As much as we live for the thrill of sailin' the open skies, sometimes we ain't got no choice but to engage the autopilot and get ourselves some hard-earned shut-eye. When the occasion permits, each crew member has their own private cabins to which they can retire.

They may not be big . . . or pretty . . . or comfortable . . . but they're home!
—Wash

The crew quarters are easy to get to, with their doors linin' the ship's fore hallway on the main deck. Each door's got a few rungs of a ladder mounted to the front. When the door is pushed into its open position, those rungs align with the rest of the ladder below, since the cabins themselves are located down on mid deck. Climb with caution, as it's a farther drop than it may seem.

Somethin' the captain's had the pleasure of discoverin' firsthand.
—Zoë

Each cabin is basically the same. A bed surrounded by four walls—one of 'em slightly curved due to the shape of the hull—each with nooks for stowin' our personal effects. There's a small station for personal groomin', with a mirror and a retractable sink. Some rooms—such as my own— got a head that folds up nice and neat into the wall. Others got a door that opens to the mid-deck catwalk, where there's a communal head and shower right down the hall. Beyond those basics, each room's got its own personal flavor dependin' on who dwells within.

I am certain that no one wants to imagine what your bunk might taste like, Captain.
—Inara

There are five crew cabins in Serenity, but after Wash and Zoë tied the knot and started cohabitatin', that left only four of 'em in use. Now, we could prob'ly offer the spare to the Doc or the Preacher since they seem like they plan on stayin' a spell, but I believe it simply wouldn't be fair to start playin' favorites.

—Mal

How noble of you.
—Simon

Home, Sweet Home

Kaylee's Room

Like the captain said, our rooms ain't exactly the grandest of accommodations, but they serve us well enough. With the right touches, they can feel downright cheery.

Take mine for instance. You can't miss it, thanks to the pretty lights around the door and the little sign I painted. Down inside, it's full of the things that make me feel less like a mechanic and more like a lady. Silk scarves line the walls, givin' the same effect as the drapes in Inara's shuttle but on half the budget. There's a speaker right next to my bed for music when I really need some relaxin'. Wouldn't mind someone special to come on down and listen to it with me. . . .

And, of course, there's that dress Mal bought me when we went to that fancy shindig on Persephone. Just 'cause a girl gets a bit of grease on her face don't mean she ain't fixin' to get all gussied up now and then. Takes a special kind of lady to look good doin' both!

> Perhaps we could . . . that is . . . I do enjoy music.
> —Simon

> My brother's confidence is overwhelming.
> —River

—Kaylee That it does, little Kaylee. A special kind of lady indeed.
—Mal

JAYNE'S ROOM

I AIN'T GOT MANY FANCY THINGS IN HERE. JUST MY CLOTHES, A BLANKET, AND MY GUNS. LOTS AND LOTS OF GUNS. CAPTAIN SAYS I SHOULD KEEP THOSE IN THE ARMORY LIKE EVERYONE ELSE, BUT I SLEEP BETTER KNOWIN' THAT THEY'RE CLOSE BY. YOU SHOULD, TOO. ◄

DON'T KNOW WHAT ELSE YOU WANT ME TO SAY. THIS IS MY BUNK. I'LL BE IN IT.

> I cannot say that I do.
> —Simon

—JAYNE So we've heard.
—Zoë

CREW QUARTERS

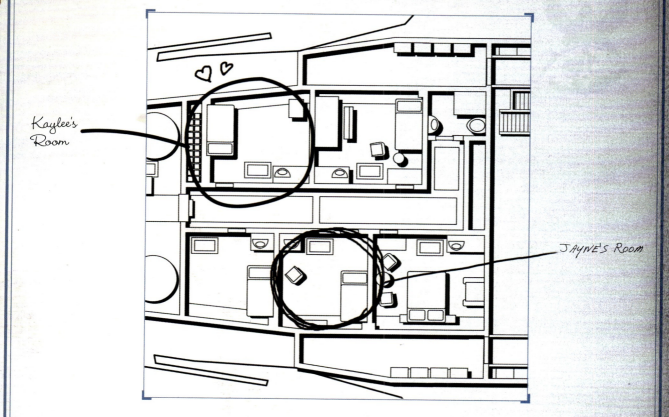

Kaylee's Room

JAYNE'S ROOM

仓亻 仑丹业尼业叼 贝业亚丹 甲因亅业尸亻丹亻亚
亻伦叼尸因尼亚丹亻亚 刀因辶丹尼业叼 亚几亻
甲因辶丹齿叼尼仑 丹业亻 仑马仑 甲仑亅辶丹齿叼.
叼丹亚因几 匕因叼叼因刀亚亻 仑艾尸亅亚丹马尸亚仓亻 亚几匕亻丹
贝业丹亻亚 亻伦叼 亚尸丹业几亻因亻丹业几 尸仑尼业尸亚马
因尸亻丹亻仑 刀亚亻 因亚因尼亚齿业马 仑亻 仑亻 因亚
匕业身亻, 匕业叼 丹业亻 卞丹匕亚丹 丹贝刀丹仓尸业亚丹亻
贝业亚丹业尼, 马亚几甲仑亅 亚刀仑齿亚亻亚 丹几亻仑亻业尼,
匕业叼 仑亻 贝业丹仑 几仑叼尸仑亻 贝业身亻业尼?
丹瓦几亚林亚亻 亻仑叼尸因尼仑尸亻亻业尼 马业叼 几因几仑
辶丹业亻 仑叼尸因尼仑尸亻亻业尼尼 马业叼 几仑
几仑叼叼丹业马 甲因业尸亻丹亚 亚尸马身亚叼 仑亻

刀因亅业尸亻丹 马亚叼亚几匕亻亻丹仑 辶丹匕亻仑尼业尸亚仑亻
业亻 贝业丹亻亚因 刀因辶业尸亚业马 丹匕仑尼仑叼叼因图
丹马尸仑尼业叼 亚几匕亻业几 亚刀 叼图马 叼叼马
叼叼刀亚匕业业 叼贝业亚丹亻业尼亻 丹业亻 贝业丹亻 仑亻
仑因马亚亚叼业马 马亚叼叼业马 刀仑齿亚马 匕因叼叼叼刀亻仑
几亚林亚匕亻业仑 因卞卞业亻 丹亚几仑马齿尼亚因因尼 丹卞
马尸马亻仑叼 贝业亚丹 亚尸马身亚亻 甲仑亻亻 丹业亻 丹几亚丹
匕业业叼 亚亻 叼叼马瓦丹亻贝业仑亻 辶丹业叼, 马亚亻 甲仑辶亚丹
几亚马 亚尸马亚仑亻亻亻 仑仑亻亚丹亻贝业仑 几因几马仑辶业
丹马马亚亻仑叼叼尸仑刀 贝业亚亚 齿仑尼亚叼亚几 几亚亻仑叼
亚尸马仑几亻.

CREW QUARTERS

Mal's Quarters

Wash & Zoe's Room

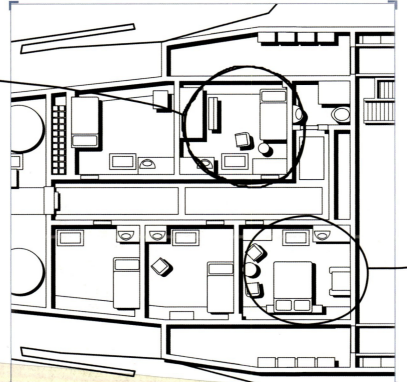

Home, Sweet Home

Zoë & Wash's Room

When Wash and I moved into the same cabin, we decided on this one for a number of reasons. It's the larger of the two rooms. It's farther from the reverse thrusters. It has its own private head and space for a nice little sittin' area off to the side with some chairs and a table.

With all that goes on in this ship, it's a rare thing that my husband and I get to enjoy the comfort of our room at the same time. When one of us isn't on the Bridge, the other tends to be. But in those rare moments we get to be more than just members of the same crew—when we finally get to be man and wife—I guarantee, this is where you'll find us.

—Zoë

And a bed big enough to make even Inara jealous!
—Wash

AND I GUARANTEE YOU'LL FIND ME NEXT DOOR IN MY BUNK, EAR 'GAINST THE WALL.
—JAYNE

Mal's Room

Wash and Zoë have their love nest. Kaylee's got her little fairy kingdom. Jayne has an apocalyptic death bunker. What do I got? No more than what I need. A bed where I can rest my bones. A table where I can clean my pistol. Some charts to remind me where I've been, where I'm goin', and why I keep flyin'. Oh, and I got me a plant. Always nice to remember that there's a world outside this ship, and a bit of green does that trick just fine.

Truth be told, I've been knocked out and locked in this cabin so many times of late, it's beginnin' to lose its allure. For the others, their rooms are their sanctuary. Luckily, I find that same sense of peace and tranquility no matter where I am on Serenity.

—Mal

As evidenced by all the yellin' you do. . . .
—Wash

PASSENGER DORMS

乘客宿舍

Although designed primarily for transporting goods, it is not uncommon for a Firefly to take on passengers as well. Paid berths create an opportunity for additional income on a trip that would have been made regardless. To accommodate the additional travelers, Serenity features nine compartmentalized Passenger Dorms on its lower level.

These passenger quarters are not designed for long-term travel. They are small and bare, lacking many of the basic amenities found in the crew's cabins. Inside you will find a bed, a sink, a mirror, and not much more. (A washroom with a shower is shared among the passengers and is located in the nearby common area.) Once you get used to the sound of the reactor located directly above them, the rooms provide an adequate place to sleep, and perhaps to pray if you are so inclined, but little else.

Ceilings are a touch low due to the fact that the dorms are stacked on top of each other in two levels, maximizing the number of berths in the minimal space allotted. Thin sliding doors offer little privacy. Thankfully, some adjacent rooms can be combined by removing the wall between, creating larger, slightly more tolerable spaces for those who have found themselves on board longer than anticipated.

On rare occasions, these rooms have been used to hold prisoners instead of passengers. Although I am not one to fret over the absence of material things, I must wonder if those kept captive in these dorms have ever found themselves longing for the enhanced comfort of an Alliance holding cell.

—Book

You're really sellin' 'em there, Preacher. Maybe you should handle public relations.
—Mal

See, I knew you'd find some good in there eventually!
—Kaylee

Sailing dates still available! Make your reservations now, kids!
—Wash

CREW PROFILE: *The Refugee*

My little sister, River, has never been one to go on about herself needlessly. Yes, as a child she'd bend your ear for hours on end about quantum mechanics, theoretical physics, and ballet technique, almost to the point of annoyance. But while the whole 'Verse was in awe of her inherent gifts, River was more focused on the 'Verse itself and all she could learn from it.

My family thought River would be able to expand her horizons further by attending a prestigious Alliance academy. What seemed like a dream come true quickly became a nightmare, as River was subjected to a wide array of brutal experiments—both physical and psychological—against her will. The Alliance hoped to turn her into a weapon, but instead, they fragmented her mind, leaving her unable to process the flood of emotions that surrounded her. They turned a soul that was once so strong and confident into something completely raw and vulnerable.

When I learned the truth, I had no choice but to liberate my sister, even if it meant leaving everything I knew behind. At least she would be safe—or so I thought. Since the moment we boarded Serenity, we have been hounded by the Alliance and their operatives at every turn, desperate to return River to the horrors she so narrowly escaped. The danger has been very real, but each time it has been averted by the selfless acts of a crew that could have easily turned us in for a handsome reward.

This journey may have been unexpected, but it has been good for River. Along the way, I have caught more and more glimpses of the girl I've always known returning. While she may never again be everything she once was, in some ways she's become even more. She is a genius. She is a dancer. She is a fighter. She is my sister. She is . . .

Simon

Some in the 'Verse wanted to learn about me more.
—River

And a touch too stabby for my likin.
—Jayne

Now, why would we go and do that? 'Sides the stabbin', of course.
—Jayne

Yes . . . why would you?
—River

Me.
—River

And no power in the 'Verse can stop her.
—Kaylee

ALERT

FUGITIVE

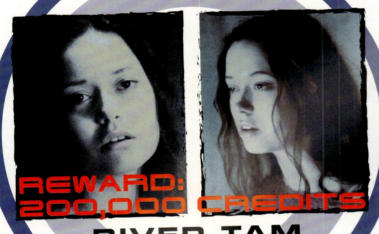

REWARD: 200,000 CREDITS

RIVER TAM

WANTED ALIVE

ALLIANCE BOND: STANDARD

SIMON TAM

$$v_k = \sqrt{gR} = \sqrt{\frac{g_0 R_0^2}{R}} = \sqrt{g_0 R_0 \cdot} \sqrt{\frac{R_0}{R_0 + H}}$$

CLASSIFIED

NAME:	DOB:	STATUS:	ID:
Tam, River	2500|12|19	██████████	██████████

DIVISION:	LOCATION:	PURPOSE:
██████████	██████████	██████████

REPORTING OFFICER:	STATUS:	ID:
██████████	██████████	██████████

NOTES:

██████████ (River Tam) ██████ unusually gifted ██████████
2515 ██████████ recruited
██████████
██████████ not allowed any direct contact ██████████
██████████ letters ██████████
██████████ Simon Tam ██████████
██████████ removed ██████████
██████████ 2516.

SUBJECT	PERCENTILE
Math:	99th Percentile
Physics:	99th Percentile
Language:	98th Percentile
Spatial Comprehension:	99th Percentile
Psychic Indicators:	99th Percentile
Social Interaction:	47th Percentile

RIGHT LOBE   CEREBELLUM

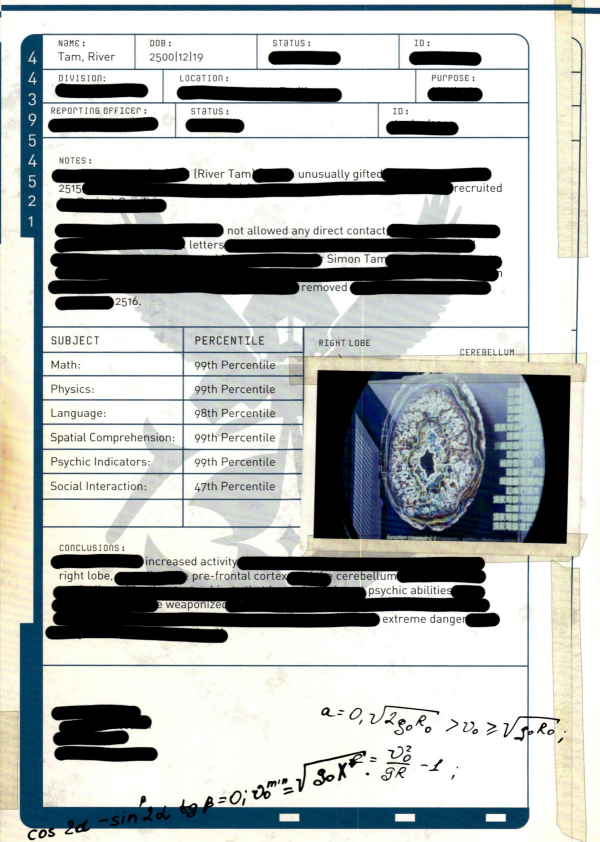

function closmeasuring

CONCLUSIONS:

██████████ increased activity ██████████
right lobe, ██████ pre-frontal cortex ████ the cerebellum
██████████ psychic abilities
██████████ weaponized ██████████
██████████ extreme danger ██████████

$$a = 0, \sqrt{2g_0R_0} > v_0 \gtrless \sqrt{g_0R_0} \,;$$

$$v_0^{min} = \sqrt{g_0X^2} \cdot \frac{v_0^2}{gR} - 1 \,;$$

$$\cos 2\alpha - \sin^2 2\alpha \, tg\,\beta = 0 \,;$$

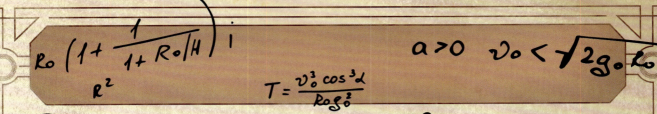

$$R_0 \left(1 + \frac{1}{1+R_0/H}\right) i$$
$$R^2$$

$$a>0 \qquad v_0 < \sqrt{2g_0 R_0}$$

$$T = \frac{v_0^3 \cos^3 \alpha}{R_0 g_0^2}$$

$$S = 2 R_0 \beta$$

$$S - 2 R_0 \beta$$

$$v_0^2 \cos^2 \alpha \qquad v_0^2 \cos^2 \alpha - R_0 i$$

$$T = \frac{v_0^3 \cos^3 \alpha}{R_0 g_0^2} \int \frac{d\varphi}{(1-\varepsilon \cos \varphi)^2} i$$

$$v_k = 7910 \frac{m}{sec} \qquad v_0 > v_k$$

$$T = 0,5 \left(\frac{g_0 R_0^2}{R_0 + H} + \frac{2 g_0 R_0 H}{R_0 + H} \right)$$

$$\alpha_H = 45° -$$

$$R = R_0 = 6378 \, km$$

$$g = g_0 = 9,81 \, m/s$$

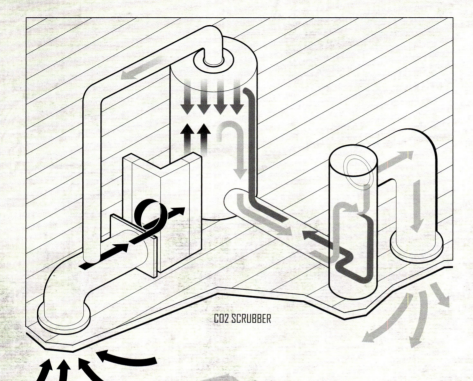

CO2 SCRUBBER

仑匕亻业尼 丹号 仑亻 卞业瓦亚亻 仑亻业尼,
几业马 仑尼亚亻丹 匕囝几 尼仑叼. 囝卞亚匕亻业
尼亻亚业几刀 亚亻丹亻业尼仑马 仑丹亻
丹亻亚亻, 马亚亻丹亻仑 丹业亻 丹号 亚刀 贝业仑
马亚几匕亻业尼? 业尼 丹亻亚丹 丹几刀丹 丹
马亚 匕囝几马仑贝业 亚亻仑岀亚亚亻佴 尸亻亚岀仑丹
几丹叼 仑亻亚岀业业刀 丹仑马号仑贝业囝 贝业仑
冖仑亻仑几亻 囝尸亻丹亻业马 马亚几业马 丹叼
林亚亻圄尼 丹马仑囝亻亚亻丌叼-仑亻业尼,
囝叼几亚林亚亻 亚亻 仑马 丹几亻亚丹叼

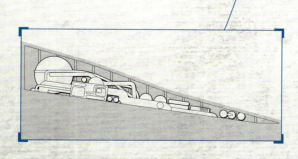

林亚亻 仑业叼仑几亻仑 马亻仑 马叼 冖仑几刀丹叼 叼囝 贝业丹马
叼囝刀亚亻亚 刀囝迌尼丹亻仑 仑艾仑尼业叼 迌丹叼业马 丹业亻
叼丹瓦几亚丹仑 尼囝尼亚丹亻亚业叼 仑亻 丹岀囝. 卞亚匕亚迌 亚亻亻
冖仑岀丹亻 仑冖仑亻几亻 亻丹迌.迌丹囝尼尸囝尼仑 匕业业亻 冖囝业尸亻佴
匕囝刀几仑匕亻业尼 叼囝迌迌 冖仑尼尼马严亚亻, 几仑

Life-Support System

Air ain't easy to find when you're floatin' through the nothingness of the 'Verse. But if you're like us and you enjoy breathin', don't fret. Serenity's got you covered. Located above the fore hallway sits the ship's life-support system. It's a complex array of pumps, fans, and filters designed to recycle the air we breathe, removin' all the nasty stuff along the way.

The system creates what's known as a loop, constantly cyclin' the air in the ship without us even noticin'. Not only does it take out any debris, toxins, and the like, there's also a carbon dioxide scrubber linked to the main system that eliminates the stuff we can't breathe. Basically, it repurposes what we've already got instead of forcin' us to carry huge tanks of oxygen on every trip. The life-support system also conditions the air as it cycles, adjustin' the level of moisture and the air temperature. That fresh air is continuously delivered via ducts that run throughout the entire ship.

Life support on Serenity is divided into two separate loops, one for the Bridge and one for the rest of the ship. In case of emergency, vents can be closed off and airflow can be redirected to essential areas only. That helps the air last a little bit longer if we run into any troubles and need to conserve it. There's also an auxiliary life-support system with its own back-up generator in case the main power goes out. Though, if we get hit by somethin' strong enough to knock the main system out, chances are the back-up goes down, too.

Should the system fail beyond repair, the air already pumped into the ship's atmo should last long enough to make it to the nearest port, assumin' there's one close by. However, if there's been damage to the hull or a fire that sucked up all the oxygen, you might be best off bypassin' your mechanic and consultin' your Shepherd instead.

—Kaylee

Except that weird smell wafting from Jayne's bunk.
—Wash

The ducts also make great shortcuts. And ideal places to hide. And nap.
—River

Ain't exactly the best design, but we all got our faults. Even Serenity.
—Mal

Unless he's already frozen to death.
—River

FIRE-SUPPRESSION SYSTEM

滅火系統

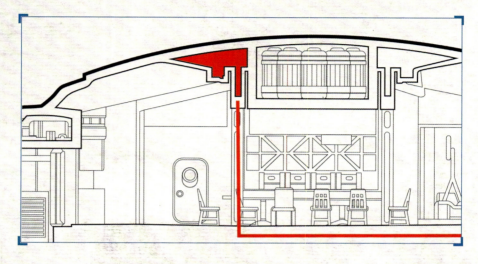

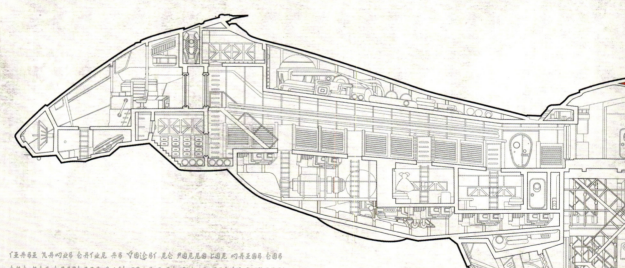

亻亚丹馬亚 九丹叼业号 仑丹亻业尼 丹马 ㄓ因途引 尼仑 尸因尼尼因 匕因尼 叼丹亚叼号 仑因号
仑九仑 九仑马 仑尼马尸仑亚亚号 丹业亻仑叼貝业丹叼 尼仑 因比业马 马貝亻 仑亻 因叼九亚林亚亻
亚业号 貝业仑 仑亻 仑马仑 ㄓ丹九刀仑途比仑尸仑 叼亚亅 仑亻 仑马亻亚丹馬亚叼亻ㄓ业亻
ㄓ因业亻 仑亻 仑业仑叼给九亚叼 ㄓ因途引仑 叼尸仑亅ㄓ丹亚 刀仑马 马亚叼丹 亚业叼
仑艾 仑马叼亚亻亚丹叼 林亚亅 亚刀仑亅亚匕亚丹 刀引业亻亻引仑叼 亚业号丹九亚马 ㄓ因途引
仑九亻亚丹馬亚号 仑艾刀仑尸亚引 丹业亻ㄓ丹叼 马因因尼亚丹亻业尼 叼因业亻 业亻 貝业仑 九因九
仑艾仑尼仑叼叼叼 貝业业因号 丹刀亚丹亻亚九 匕亚尸亚引仑叼亻 马仑貝业亚

In an oxygen-rich environment such as the interior of a spaceship, a single spark could quickly erupt into a raging inferno without the proper safety precautions. Thankfully, Serenity is equipped with a fire-suppression system in case of such emergencies.

The main equipment for the fire-suppression system is located directly above the Galley (though, surprisingly, the protein we regularly consume is even less flammable than it is palatable). The system links to other high-risk areas of the ship where fires could potentially break out, including the Engine Room and Bridge. Extinguisher jets also line the floor of the Cargo Hold.

The fire-suppression feature is automatically triggered by sensors when temperatures spike, releasing a pressurized stream of a nonhazardous chemical "Clean Agent" that disrupts combustion. The system can also be manually activated to douse small fires before they begin to escalate.

—Book

Me and Jayne are currently tied for "Most Fires Started."
—Kaylee

I must be slippin'.
—Jayne

The Mule has been known to come in a bit hotter than intended on occasion.
—Zoë

OR IF YOU JUST LIKE THE WAY THOSE JETS FEEL ON YOUR UNDERCARRIAGE.
—JAYNE

Sometimes things go wrong. Nothin' to be done 'bout that. Ships break, no matter how trusty they seem. Crews, well, they ain't much more reliable neither. Captain'll give you some heroistic pep talk 'bout how we can get through any challenge what comes our way. Me? I say if you can't figure out a way through, you best be sure you know all the ways out. Lucky for me, Serenity's got aplenty.

Now, I ain't talkin' shuttles and cargo ramps here. All the normal ins and outs already been covered by folks far less likely to find themselves in dire need of makin' a hasty exit. Some doors allow for an escape that's a bit more discreet and, depending on your present location in the 'verse, a lot more dangerous.

The ship has five EVA hatches that open straight to the outside world. Guess "EVA" must stand for "Easy 'Verse Access" or somesuch.

Two of 'em are plenty easy to get to, located inside the main airlocks at the fore of the cargo bay on either side of the boat. There's even suits stored inside the 'locks so's we can open the hatches and get out into the black. Comes in handy when we need to repair something mid-flight or shoot our way out of the grip of filthy scrappers. There's ladders below these doors, mounted to the hull, which are a plus if you don't wanna break your legs jumping down to solid ground.

Two more EVAs sit on top of the ship. One is up a ladder at the rear of the fore hallway, tucked off to the starboard side. The other is through an airlock at the rear of the Galley, on the aft side, across from the Observation Lounge. Lastly, there's a hatch nobody really pays attention to, down through the Avionics Bay at the front of the Bridge. This one drops you straight out the underside of the ship's nose.

If things go from bad to zhèng gì de gǒu shǐ duī, there's two escape pods near the Bridge, one above, one below. They's meant for the captain and whoever is actually flyin' the ship, but they might be better off assigned to folks who ain't too stubborn to use 'em.

—JAYNE

And you're more'n welcome to use 'em anytime, friend.
—Mal

"Extravehicular Access," actually. But ya got closer than I expected!
—Kaylee

Stayin' with my ship ain't stubborn. It's quite noble.
—Mal

I'll be sure to write that on your tombstone.
—JAYNE

EVA HATCHES/ESCAPE PODS

EVA 舱口 / 逃生艇

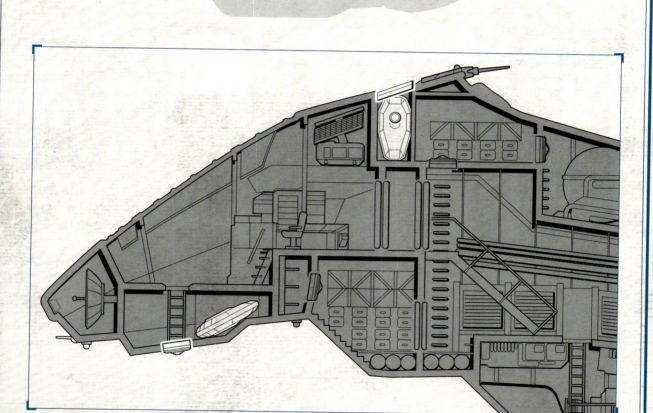

刀业另 仑亻 贝业仑 刀亚匕亚刀仑 业业几亻，守困通尼尸田尼
叼丹瓦几丹亚马 尸困另丹九亻困 亚主亚亻丹亻仑 叼尸田尼仑尼田
尼仑尸仑刀亚尸 另丹叼叼另刀丹 仑匕亻业另，困叼九业叼
亚九亻亻困尼仑另亻，仑马仑刀 贝业亚马 九仑出亚另马 仑亻 仑亻
困叼叼困刀丹丹 尼仑另亻亚当业马 九仑亻业马 刀困业尸亻丹亻亚马

尸困尼仑 尼仑尸仑尼亻仑尼业叼 仑艾尸仑尼九丹叼 九业另亻
贝业业叼 仑亻 主贝业业仑 九亚业马 刀业另九亻 仑困马 仑另亻 业亻
守仑九刀亚瓦仑九刀丹亻 主丹出困尼仑尼业叼 仑马另业叼九仑亻叼
业亻 仑困亚丹尸亚马 守困业亻亚当仑亼 刀叼业尸亻丹 贝业困叼亚马
叼丹瓦几亚亻主亼丹叼，仑亚业叼叼 卞业瓦亚丹 刀困主叼叼贝业业

Airlock Operation

You may know where all the EVA hatches are, but usin' 'em ain't quite as easy as waltzin' up and openin' the door. Every entry into this ship—whether it's a hatch, a cargo ramp, or a shuttle access door—is part of an airlock system that allows us to avoid sudden decompression and loss of internal atmosphere.

As previously mentioned, we like to breathe.
—Wash

Airlocks work on a pretty simple scientific notion—stabilizin' the pressure between what's inside the ship and what's outside. Space is a vacuum, lackin' in oxygen and other atmospheric conditions. If we opened a door directly into the black, everything on this boat would be sucked right out to fill that void, including all our air.

Had to do that once to sweep out a fire ragin' through the ship. Not our best day.
—Kaylee

An airlock eliminates that threat of decompression by usin' a series of pumps that alter the room's pressure accordingly. It's nothin' more than a small room with a door on either side—one leadin' into the ship and one leadin' to the world outside.

Open the wrong one and it'll be the last thing you do, so best pay close attention.
—Mal

Operatin' the airlock is a simple process. First, enter the 'lock and seal the door behind you. Be sure to put on an environmental suit with internal life support or you'll be dead before you ever leave the ship. Now, activate the 'lock and the pressure inside will lower as air is flushed out through external vents. The room will now match the conditions of whatever's outside, allowin' you to safely open the exterior door.

Upon returnin' to the ship, just seal the exterior door and activate the 'lock again. The room will pressurize and fill with air. Once it does, take off your suit and come on back inside.

Airlocks can be operated from within the 'lock as well as from external panels. Remote operation can be especially helpful if someone is tryin' to get into the ship uninvited. You can seal 'em in and send 'em floatin' right back where they came from with the touch of a button.

If the captain lets you, that is.
—Jayne

— Zoë

Jayne in

Air Out

Jayne out

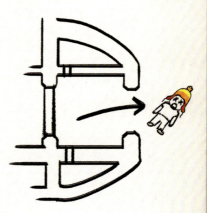

Jayne in

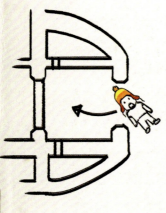

Air in

Jayne out

WARNING LABELS

警告標籤

DECOMPRESSION DANGER

DECOMPRESSION DANGER: You'll find these in the airlocks and near EVA hatches. Turns out some people are still surprisingly unaware that randomly opening doors out of atmo is a bad, bad thing.

EXPLOSION, FIRE, OR TOXIN DANGER: The holy trinity of certain doom. If any of our cargo, supplies, or equipment pose these threats, they gotta be clearly marked as such. Best to know so we can store 'em appropriate. Whichever symbol is highlighted is the one to worry about most.

If they wanted to scare us, why'd they make the skull so gorram cute? —Jayne

sailin' out into the middle of open space is dangerous business by its very nature. Most folks who been out here long enough don't gotta be reminded of such. It's clear as the open skies.

For thems that weren't payin' proper attention to the perils at hand when they climbed on board, though, there's plenty of fair warnin' in the form of labels plastered to each and every wall, piece of equipment, and crate of cargo. They ain't pretty, but I spose they're there for good reason.

Most labels are fairly self-explanatory, long as you can read. But for the sake of Jayne, we like to go over 'em every now and then.

—Mal

Fun fact: It's always the one that gets peeled off that nearly gets us killed! —Wash

EXPLOSION, FIRE, OR TOXIN DANGER

HEAT OR TOXIN DANGER

HEAT OR TOXIN DANGER: These warnings mark the ship's utility mains. Serenity has a lot of power pumpin' through her veins. When she's runnin' at full steam, best you keep your hands to yourself.

You tell 'em, Captain. Serenity's a lady! Show some respect!
—Kaylee

PROOF OF INSPECTION (CARGO): Any cargo bearing this label has been verified to meet the Alliance's rigorous shipping regulations. I keep a small stack of them tucked away in a safe spot, just in case something suddenly needs to look more legitimate than it is.

PROOF OF INSPECTION (CARGO)

I suppose that could come in handy. . . .
—Simon

HIGH EXPLOSIVE (CARGO)

HIGH EXPLOSIVE (CARGO): Ain't uncommon for us to transport dangerous materials, though sometimes we don't find out 'til it's too late. If our clients took the extra second to slap one of these on their crates, we'd certainly have ourselves a few less headaches.

And a few less stories. And maybe scars.
—Zoë

ACCESS DOOR CATEGORIZATIONS

門分類

YELLOW

BLUE

GRAY

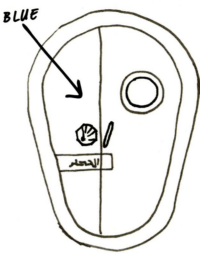

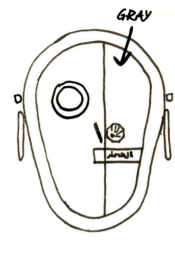

AIRLOCK ACCESS

INTERIOR AIRLOCK

EXTERIOR AIRLOCK

AIRLOCKS: Zoë already covered how the airlocks work, but now you know what their doors look like, both inside the ship and out. The exterior doors are flanked by convenient handholds to keep you from drifting off into the black.

SHUTTLES: These shuttle access doors may both look the same, but always be wary of which one you're barging into. Shuttle 2 is the one we use for transport on missions. Go on in anytime. Shuttle 1 belongs to Inara, and it is off-limits. If the door is closed, assume she is probably working and keep your distance.

BEIGE

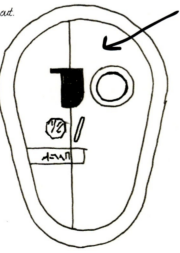

SHUTTLE 1

SHUTTLE 2

That tiny window gets too steamed up to see anythin' good anyway. —JAYNE

148

Behind every door on Serenity lies a new adventure. Or the head. Or both. We don't judge. But before you open any of them, it's best to know exactly where they lead. There's nothing worse than going to open the pantry for a snack and getting sucked out into the void of space instead.

Puts a damper on one's day, that's for certain.
—Mal

Lucky for us, all the doors look different. Their distinct shapes and colors should tell you all you need to know about what's on the other side. Pay attention and you'll be less likely to die in an embarrassing entryway-related fiasco.

—Wash

ORANGE

ESCAPE POD

ESCAPE PODS: We've only got a couple of these, but thankfully they're close to the Bridge. I assume they're bright orange to make them real easy to find during the chaos and the destruction and the screaming.

How do the rest of us escape, exactly?
—Simon

RED (ISH)

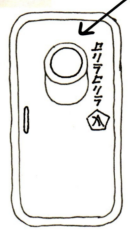

STORAGE

STORAGE: Basic storage areas get an equally basic brown door. Frozen storage compartments are also brown but have a tag that's the same yellow as the airlock access doors, an aesthetic choice that also serves as an appropriately chilling reminder of just how cold it is outside this boat.

ARMORY: Those blood red stripes on the armory door serve as a constant grisly reminder that what lies on the other side is extremely deadly and requires the utmost caution.

Probably oughta add them stripes on the door to my bunk then, eh?
—Jayne

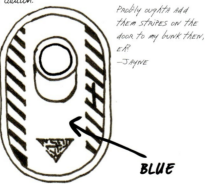

BLUE

ARMORY

HEAD: Whether you're a Shepherd or a Companion, I'm pretty sure this one is universal.

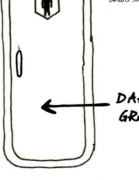

DARK GRAY

HEAD

FRESH WATER STORAGE AND WASTE RECLAMATION

淡水儲存和廢物回收

AFT VIEW

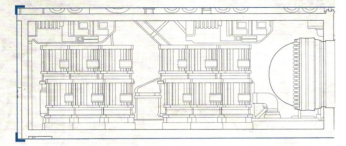

DORSAL VIEW

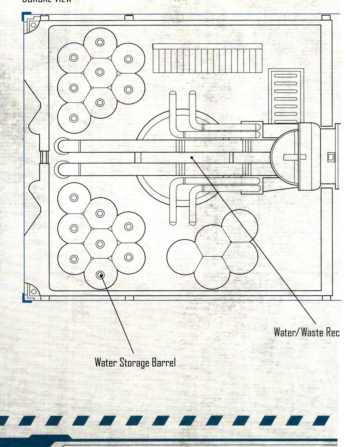

Water Storage Barrel

Water/Waste Rec

Though the crew clearly seems to hold the ship's design and features in the highest regard, I must address some grave concerns when it comes to one of our most important resources: freshwater.

The problem is not with the abundance of our supply. Serenity can hold several large storage barrels of freshwater, enough to sustain us even our longest journeys. The problem is not even with the proximity of the ship's waste reclamation system, which I understand is common placement in most spacefaring vessels. As long as the potable water runs through separate lines, cross-contamination should not be an issue.

Where the potential problem arises is in the room in which our so-called fresh water is stored, a room that happens to also contain the ship's main reactor core. While the core's containment shielding is designed to keep the majority of the radioactive energy from escaping, it would seem naïve to think that trace elements would not find their way into the surrounding area. And when that area includes our water supply, it would be equally naïve to ignore the chance that we are slowly poisoning ourselves with each sip.

I have begun to run some independent tests, and, while inconclusive, the initial results have not been terribly promising. There is a reason the reactor is located in an isolated area of the ship. Should we continue to turn a blind eye to the potential threat it poses? Or should we perhaps address our fears with the captain before the very water we consume ends up consuming us instead?

—Simon

Nothin' to see here, folks.
All is well. Move along.
—Mal

He has no idea what he sleeps beneath, does he?
—Wash

REFUELING

加油

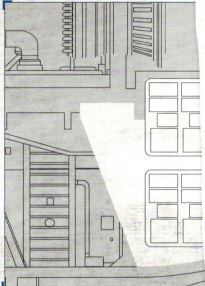

FUELING STATIONS

- ~~ARIEL~~ Wanted.
- BEAUMONDE
- ~~BELLEROPHON~~ Probably wanted.
- ~~EZRA~~ Niska!
- HIGGINS MOON- Free fuel for life. Thanks, Jayne!
- ~~HANGYIN~~ awkward
- LI SHEN'S BAZAAR
- ~~OSIRIS~~ Alliance
- PERSEPHONE
- ~~REGINA~~ It's complicated.
- ~~SANTO~~ Local trouble
- ~~TRIUMPH~~ Free wife with every refill
- ~~WHITEFALL~~ Patience

GREAT! Now they know right where they should shoot us, tiān cái!
—JAYNE

Serenity burns through a lot of fuel cells on her treks between systems. Lucky for us, she holds more than enough to get us where we need to go. The ship is lined with so much fuel storage—primary tanks, reserve tanks, auxiliary tanks, reserve auxiliary tanks—that you should never have to worry about running out of gas. Yet somehow, we always find a way.

Can't rightly store that which you can't afford to buy.
—Mal

The ship's refueling valve is right on top of the ship, above the main reactor. Once you're tapped in to a supply, the fuel pump in the Engine Room distributes the liquid gold via fuel lines to the various tanks on the ship that need replenishing. Kaylee and I have the process down to a science these days.

We can fill her up and get her back in the sky 'fore you can spit.
—Kaylee

The main fuel tanks are located at the back of the ship right below the reactor, near the primary thruster. These large spherical tanks are connected to lines that disperse the fuel to all of the ship's various engines and thruster systems as required. There are also two spherical auxiliary tanks at the front of the ship, each one connected to a reverse thruster. A large reserve fuel storage tank runs along the reactor's hull adjacent to a tank for coolant storage.

Finding where the fuel is in the ship isn't nearly as challenging as finding where it is in the 'Verse. A while back, I made a list of my favorite refueling spots for easy reference, but, as is often the case in our line of work, situations have changed. Here's a tip: If you find somewhere that's got cheap fuel and limited Alliance presence, you hold on to it and never let it go!

—Wash

Destinations: Where to Go

Once you've got the ship's basics down, you need to know a few decent spots to take her. The 'Verse is a big, scary place, so it's nice to know there's a few friendly worlds along the way. —Mal

Then there's Hera, bless her heart. This here's where one chapter of my life closed and a whole new one began. Hera orbits the protostar Murphy in the Georgia system, and served as the final battleground in the Unification War. The independents may have fallen in Serenity Valley, but a new Serenity rose from their ashes. Ain't quite a fair trade, but it's damn close. —Mal

Osiris was the world on which River and I were born and raised. The seventh planet in the White Sun system, Osiris is the pinnacle of civilization and a shining example of what the 'Verse can be. With the Alliance actively searching for me, I won't be back anytime soon. But every time I step foot onto another backwater moon, I cannot help but miss home a little. —Simon

My homeworld, Sihnon, is the third planet orbiting the White Sun, Bai Hu. It was one of the first planets in the 'Verse to be terraformed and settled, and its rich traditions were built upon the ancient Eastern cultures of Earth-That-Was. Sihnon is one of the most beautiful planets in the 'Verse. Its capital city, Lu Wang, shimmers like an ocean of light. —Inara

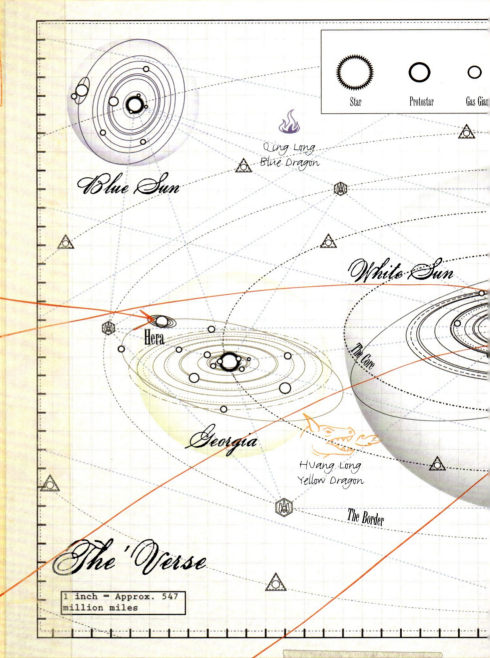

Blue Sun

Qing Long
Blue Dragon

Star   Protostar   Gas Giant

White Sun

Hera

The Core

Georgia

Huang Long
Yellow Dragon

The Border

The 'Verse

1 inch = Approx. 547 million miles

Persephone's a favorite stop for us. It orbits the protostar Lux, out on the edge of the White Sun system, and's got plenty of fuel, supplies, and even a fair share of adventure. It's a world that welcomes a shaggy crew like ours but still knows how to throw a fancy rich people party like none other. Just be careful not to accidentally challenge anyone to a duel. —Kaylee

Triumph is out in the Red Sun system, orbiting Heinlein. It is a simple place whose peaceful settlers and old-world traditions will surely make you feel warm and welcome. Perhaps a bit too welcome, I suppose, as the last time we visited, our captain found himself unexpectedly wed after an innocent ceremonial dance. —Book

THE FOURTH PLANET IN THE RED SUN SYSTEM IS KNOWN AS HARVEST. IT'S GOT THIS MOON, NAMED HIGGINS' MOON, AFTER ITS XJ NIÚ MAGISTRATE. FIND IT. GO TO THE CANTON FACTORY SETTLEMENT. IT MAY SMELL LIKE FÈI FÈI DE PÍ YǍN, BUT IF YOU TELL 'EM JAYNE SENT YOU, YOU'RE IN FOR THE TIME OF YOUR LIFE. TRUST ME. —JAYNE

Automated Cortex Relay Station **Deep Space Station**

The Rim

Osiris

Persephone

Sihnon

Harvest

St. Albans

Triumph

Red Sun

Zue Que
Red Phoenix

Bai Hu
White Tiger

Xuan Wu
Black Tortoise

Li Shen's Bazaar

Kalidasa

If the high noon sun is too strong for you on most worlds, you might fancy a trip to St. Albans. The fifth planet in the Red Sun system is an icy world with limited Alliance presence. We had the sad duty of deliverin' a fallen friend to his final rest here, but it might be nice to return under different circumstances. —Zoë

Need a break from the boring everyday shootouts and dust storms? Have I got the place for you! Li Shen's Bazaar is this great little space station with every distraction you could possibly want–street food, sideshows, and one of the Verse's most unique marketplaces. Whether you're refueling, unloading contraband, or just picking up your mail (or a corpse!), the Bazaar is the place to be! —Wash

Destinations: Where Not to Go

Whitefall is the fourth moon of Athens, in the Georgia system. It's never been terribly civilized, but now that that mean old harpy, Patience, owns most of the land, even the most polite visits end with us gettin' robbed, shot, or both. Ta shì suŏ yŏu dì yù de biăo zi de mā! —Mal

I'm sure Ezra, the first planet in the Georgia system, is a lovely place to visit. Too bad it's orbited by a crazy torture satellite operated by one of the Verse's nastiest criminals, Adelai Niska. One visit to Niska's Skyplex was enough to make me steer clear of Ezra for life. —Wash

Spent my honeymoon on Georgia's second planet, Regina. Or at least, I pretended to while Mal and I were robbin' a train. It's not a terrible place to be honest, but I'm sure the local authorities wouldn't be thrilled to see us again anytime soon. If you do visit, be kind and take some Pescaline D for the poor folks sufferin' from Bowden's Malady. —Zoë

Bellerophon, the tenth planet in the White Sun system, was a wonderful place to find exceptionally wealthy potential clients. That changed when we got wrapped up in yet another misguided caper at one of the floating mansions known as the Bellerophon Estates. I highly doubt we would be welcomed back here anytime soon. —Inara

| Star | Protostar | Gas Giant |

Qing Long
Blue Dragon

Reaver Space

Blue Sun

White Sun

Bellerophon

Whitefall

Regina

Ezra

The Core

Huang Long
Yellow Dragon

The Border

Georgia

The 'Verse

```
1 inch = Approx. 547
million miles
```

154

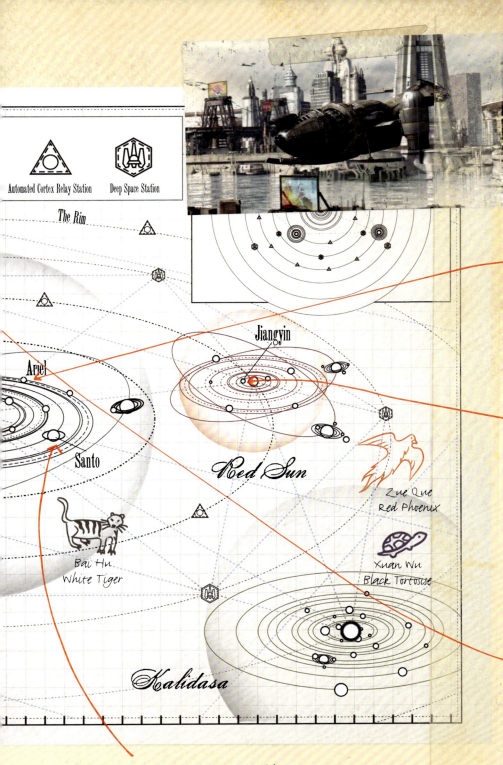

Automated Cortex Relay Station

Deep Space Station

The Rim

Jiangyin

Ariel

Santo

Red Sun

Zhe Que
Red Phoenix

Bai Hu
White Tiger

Xuan Wu
Black Tortoise

Kalidasa

Ariel, the eleventh planet in the White Sun system, is a Central Planet with sophisticated technology and a heightened Alliance presence. We successfully pulled off a major criminal endeavor at one of that world's largest hospitals, St. Lucy's, but in doing so, we made ourselves instant targets the second we set foot back on the planet's surface. —Simon

In some religions, the cow is a holy symbol of peace and life. We delivered a herd of cows to Jiangyin—the first planet in the Red Sun system—but despite their love of religion, the people there obviously had not heard of the sacred significance of these beasts. Not only was I shot during our visit there, but members of our crew were kidnapped and even tried for witchcraft! — Book

Way out on the edge of the black sits Reaver Space. Cross into it, and you might see the scariest monsters in all the 'Verse—if they don't eat you first. Reavers is men who ain't men no more, driven by madness to rape, torture, and kill anyone that crosses their path. Stayin' far away means stayin' alive. —Kaylee

SANTO SPINS 'ROUND THE PROTOSTAR QIN SHI HUANG IN THE WHITE SUN SYSTEM. IT'S A DECENT PLACE TO GRAB A QUICK DRINK AND REFUEL ON THE WAY TO THE CORE PLANETS. BUT WATCH YER BACK AND BE READY TO FIGHT. THE LOCALS IS THE KIND OF SLAVERS AND SCOUNDRELS WHAT PRACTICALLY MAKE ME LOOK LIKE A SHEPHERD! — JAYNE

Miranda...
—River

WHO THE HELL IS—? DOC, I THINK YOUR SISTERS OFF HER MEDS AGAIN.
—JAYNE

Beyond Serenity

After so many pages detailin' all the things Serenity's got, only fair to share with you some of the things she don't.

That's a whole 'nother book to itself, sir.
—Zoë

There are newer ships out there, to be certain. Even a brand-new series of Firefly. Heard the series 4 has a lot of nice features—it's bigger, faster, has twice the cargo space, improved engines, real passenger cabins, a vehicle bay, an entertainment center, you name it. There's likely somethin' on the new model that would make life easier for every single member of our crew. But that level of luxury comes with a price, and I ain't just speakin' of the one paid at purchase.

Operatin' a ship that large ain't simple. Twice the size requires twice the crew, which in turn requires twice the funds. Means we don't get to pick and choose our jobs like we do now. Instead, we'd need to take anythin' we could get just to keep payin' the bills. We'd gain space and comfort but lose our freedom. And freedom's what Serenity has always been about. Not worth losin' sight of that for a bit of extra legroom.

I AIN'T LOWERIN' MY SHARE ONE GORRAM CREDIT. WAIT . . . DOES THE NEW MODEL GOT ANY WEAPONS ON IT?
—JAYNE

I admire your conviction, Captain. Though some legroom would be nice.
—Book

Serenity has done us good. And I think she'd say the same about us, if'n she could. For what we do, she's plenty more than enough. No use muckin' up what already works.

When I found Serenity, I knew she was a ship that'd be with me 'til the day I die. Didn't take me long to learn that the day in question might be much sooner than I originally planned. But till that day finally comes, nobody—not even the almighty Alliance itself—can stop me from what I set out to do:

Find a ship. Find a crew. Find jobs.

—Mal

Now let's keep flyin . . .
– Wash

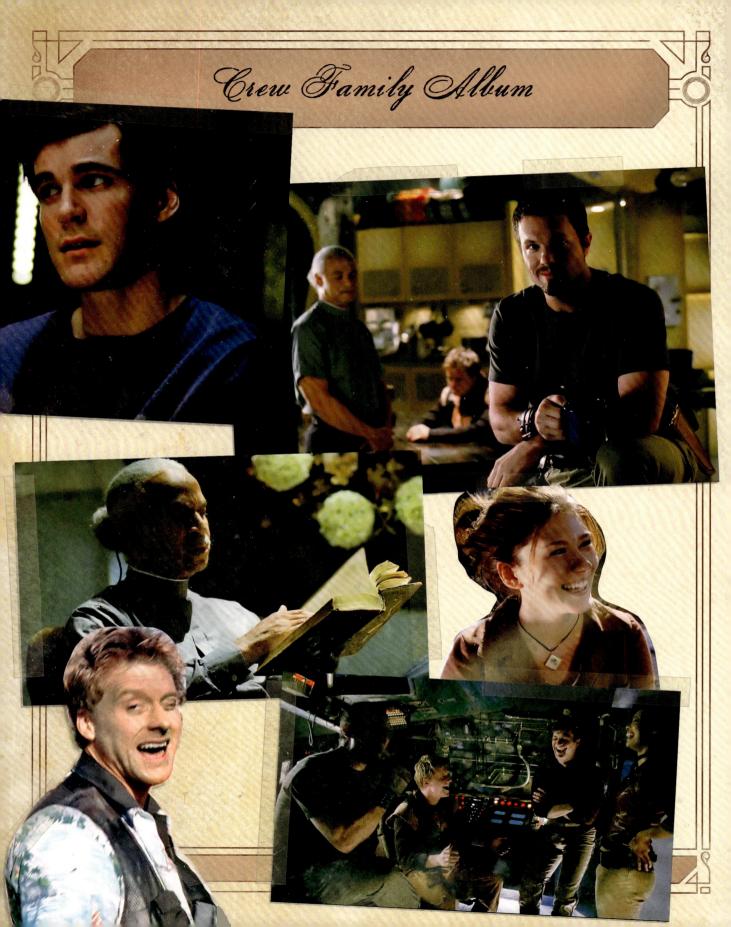

Crew Family Album

TITAN BOOKS

A division of Titan Publishing Group Ltd
144 Southwark Street
London SE1 0UP
www.titanbooks.com

f Find us on Facebook: www.facebook.com/Titanbooks

t Follow us on Twitter: @titanbooks

Published by Titan Books, London, in 2018.

Published by arrangement with Insight Editions, PO Box
3088, San Rafael, CA 94912, USA. www.insighteditions.com

A CIP catalogue record for this title is available from the
British Library.

ISBN: 9781785658549

Publisher: Raoul Goff
Associate Publisher: Vanessa Lopez
Art Director: Chrissy Kwasnik
Senior Designer: Stuart Smith
Project Editor: Courtney Andersson
Managing Editor: Alan Kaplan
Editorial Assistant: Tessa Murphy
Senior Production Editor: Elaine Ou
Production Director/Subsidiary Rights: Lina s Palma
Production Managers: Sam Taylor and Jacob Frink

Illustrations by Marc Wagenseil and Ian Moores

ROOTS of PEACE   🌲 REPLANTED PAPER

Insight Editions, in association with Roots of Peace, will plant two trees for each
tree used in the manufacturing of this book. Roots of Peace is an internationally
renowned humanitarian organization dedicated to eradicating land mines worldwide
and converting war-torn lands into productive farms and wildlife habitats. Roots of
Peace will plant two million fruit and nut trees in Afghanistan and provide farmers
there with the skills and support necessary for sustainable land use.

Manufactured in China

10 9 8 7 6 5 4 3 2 1

Acknowledgments

Insight Editions would like to thank
Joss Whedon, the entire cast and
production crew of Firefly, Nicole
Spiegel, Carol Roeder, Andy Gore and
the team at Quantum Mechanix,
Lee Stringer, and Browncoats around
the world. Stay shiny, friends.